Wisdom for Today's Family

Great wishes

John W Drakeford.

Wisdom for Today's Family

John W. Drakeford

Broadman Press
Nashville, Tennessee

© Copyright 1978 · Broadman Press
All rights reserved

4255–92

ISBN: 0–8054–5592–2

Unless otherwise noted, all Scripture quotations
in this book are from *The Living Bible, Para-
phrased* (Wheaton, Illinois: Tyndale House Pub-
lishers, 1971), and are used by permission.

Dewey Decimal Classification: 223.7
Subject Heading: BIBLE. O. T. PROVERBS // FAMILY
Library of Congress Catalog Number: 77–94449
Printed in the United States of America

PREFACE

In many fields of teaching, students often take pleasure in noting their professor was a certain great personality and will often say with obvious pride, "I studied under Dr. Carl Rogers, Dr. Allport, Dr. Sullivan, Dr. O. Hobart Mowrer," or some other noted teacher. I have been given to this sort of braggadocio myself, dropping the names of outstanding teachers with whom I've had even some remote association. But the moment of truth is here, and experiences across the years now cause me to confess that of all the teachers I have studied under, none was more innovative, provocative, and stimulating than the man who gave us the marvelous body of writing known as the book of Proverbs.

It all began in the late 1930's. Following a dramatic conversion experience in Sydney, Australia, I had learned of an educational institution in the USA that taught courses in Christian work. I wrote off and enrolled. I'll never forget the excitement when, after what seemed an age, the mailman delivered a letter which on the envelope—in typical American p.r. style—stated: "The sun never sets on our students." As I did my assignments, regularly and conscientiously, one called for me to tell of my goals and ambitions. With all the enthusiasm of the newly converted, I poured out the story of my fond aspirations. After what seemed like an eternity I received back my corrected assignment and in comment on my fervent statements of my goals the instructor had written a Scripture reference, Proverbs 3:5–6. I hurried over to my Bible and read the words, "Trust in the Lord with all thine heart; and lean not unto thine own understanding. In all thy ways acknowledge him and he shall direct thy paths."

Some ten years later I was in my first post-seminary church. Among our members was a saintly woman who, with her foundry-worker husband, had organized a Sunday School, built a building on their own property, and was ministering to hundreds of children. I knew of their limited means. One day I commended the marvelous work she was doing but wondered aloud about how they were able to put up a building, buy supplies, keep the operation going, and look on towards retirement. That sweet, saintly woman looked at me and responded, "A good name is rather to be chosen than great riches" (Proverbs 22:1, KJV).

Some ten years later, at the time of life in which most sensible people settled down, we uprooted our family and moved some 10,000 miles to start an entirely new life in the United States. A student again, I sat at the feet of Dr. J. M. Price, the founder of Southwestern Baptist Seminary's School of Religious Education. Dr. Price, who could recall teaching classes in the hills of Kentucky when a revolver clattered to the floor from a pupil's pocket, and the days of teaching in classrooms in Indian territory, later to be called Oklahoma, was the master of the art of the anecdote. His lectures were embroidered with folksy stories, homespun philosophy, and witty asides. As he discussed teaching and counseling, he revelled in the book of Proverbs. He often speculated as to the types of problems the

Proverbial counselor faced. Obviously, personal virtues were mentioned, "He that ruleth his spirit [is better] than he that taketh a city" (Proverbs 16:32, KJV). The business-man of the day apparently talked with the wise man about his struggles in the world of commerce, and insight into some of these is given by the statement, 'Utterly worth-less!' says the buyer as he haggles over the price. But after-wards he brags about his bargain!" (Proverbs 20:14).

Dr. Price, a master teller of tales, would add that family counseling was a part of the wise men's activities. Then, with that peculiar little smile that alerted his students of a humorous twist about to follow, he would quote, "It is better to dwell in a corner of the house top, than with a brawling woman in a wide house" (Proverbs 21:9).

Later I came in contact with *The Living Bible* whose colloquial style provided a wonderful vehicle for these pithy proverbial statements repeated by common people. As I read and reread the Proverbs in *The Living Bible* I was struck by the frequent reference to family life. I came up with the idea that these would be a useful guide for family living and the family devotional book, *A Proverb a Day Keeps the Troubles Away*, was the first fruits of my en-counter with *The Living Bible*.

I moved on to other writing projects, but the rela-tionship of Proverbs to family life continued to haunt me. In odd moments I turned back to this idea and finally gave it my undivided attention—as a writing project, that is—as I worked in teaching and directing the workings of a thriv-ing marriage and family counseling center. The parallels between this ancient writing and the twentieth-century prob-lems we faced in the center were striking and spurred me on in the task of applying proverbial teachings to family life today.

One difficulty with *The Living Bible* was accessi-bility. It seemed as if there were no concordance to help in locating the proverbs scattered throughout the book like gems in a field. But there *was* a concordance, a volume that had a peculiar connection with family life. The saga commenced with the premature birth of a two-pound Martin Fuller Speer on November 25, 1972. In the midst of his concern about his baby boy's survival, Jack Speer, his father, found much help from reading the easily understood *Living Bible*. As the child hung tenuously to life, then began to grow and develop, Jack Speer with a computer-library background conceived the idea of producing a concordance to *The Living Bible*, and suggested to the fifty-eight-member Poolsville Presbyterian Church that they print and publish the concordance. The finished volume has a dedication which reads:

> *Dedicated to God through the miracle*
> *of Martin Fuller Speer*

It is appropriate that the main biblical quotes of this writing should come from *The Living Bible* with its colloquial language and to which access is gained through a concordance that was compiled as a result of what a group of people came to see as a family miracle.

Like the proud student bragging about his relationship with his professor, I want to boast about the time I spent with my teacher. With Solomon I've looked at troubled parents, worried businessmen, rebellious children, the tactics of ladies of the evening, the ineptness of politicians, the jealousy, crankiness, nagging, loveliness, fidelity, energy, business acumen of women, the disciplining of children, the glory of old age. Like the Queen of Sheba in a bygone day, after spending so much time in Solomon's company, I want to exclaim, "The half hath not been told."

CONTENTS

1

A MEMORABLE VERDICT

Mrs. Carter, after filling out an information form, sat at last in the interviewing room opposite the handsome young counselor who asked, "Why don't you tell me all about it?" The middle-aged mother of three heistated for a moment before verbalizing her apprehensions, "I hardly know where to start. I've never been to a marriage counselor before. They didn't have them when I was a girl." The counselor responded, "Marriage counseling *is* a very new profession."

While marriage counseling may be a new profession it is certainly not a new activity. In some form it was carried on as far back as 1000 B.C. by people who specialized in counseling. The prophecy of Jeremiah says, "For the law shall not perish from the priest, nor counsel from the wise nor the word from the prophet" (Jeremiah 18:18). From this we can conclude that the intellectual class of ancient Israel was spoken of as priests, prophets, and the wise. The function of the priest was to give instruction; the prophet, to give the word; and the wise, to give counsel. These wise men performed the functions of teacher and counselor, these two roles overlapping and intermingling. Significant to this day, counseling in many ways is best seen as an educational program.

The appearance of a class of people known as the "wise" along with the priests and prophets was an indication that a new movement was reaching its peak. For years there had been a growing respect for people who were able to help others solve their problems. In the king's court certain individuals were achieving wide reputations because of their capacity to help troubled individuals. In King David's entourage a roll call of significant people in his kingdom included, "The attendant to the King's son was Jonathan, David's uncle, *a wise counselor* and educated man . . . Ahithophel was the *king's counselor:* and Hushai and the Archite was his *personal advisor*" (1 Chronicles 27: 32–33).

King David himself was gifted with some unusual capacities for helping people, and as a youth had been of considerable assistance to King Saul. As Saul struggled with severe emotional problems, his servants tactfully reminded him of David's reputation for helping people. The youth was summoned to the court of the king where he speedily developed a close relationship with the troubled monarch. As David played the harp he used some elemental type of music therapy that calmed Saul's troubled spirit and helped him cope with his depression. In the relationship that followed, David demonstrated a certain psychological expertise in the way he handled the violent demonstrations of the demented king.

David was apparently familiar with many of the indications of psychosis and neurosis. When in danger from Achish King of Gath and looking for a way of escape, he pretended to be in a psychotic condition. "So he pretended to be insane! He scratched on doors and let his spittle flow down his beard, until finally King Achish said to his men,

'Must you bring me a madman? We already have enough of them around here! Should such a fellow as this be my guest?' " (1 Samuel 21:13–15). The impersonation of madness was so apt it becomes evident that David from his close contacts with troubled people was knowledgable in recognizing and portraying psychotic symptoms.

Later when David needed some specific counsel to help him concerning relationships with his son, Absalom, he may have recalled his own experiences and decided to get help, "He sent for a woman of Tekoa who had a reputation for great wisdom" (2 Samuel 14:2).

The concept of community mental health programs is generally thought of as being an innovation of modern times. Instead of separating people from their families and sending them off to distant institutions, an effort is being made to keep them within their own communities, in community mental health centers where they can maintain their ties with family and friends. Perhaps the wisdom movement somehow anticipated this emphasis for, in the days of the wise men, there were certain communities that enjoyed high reputations for their ability to help troubled people. The town of Abel was apparently such a place for of it was said, "There used to be a saying, 'If you want to settle an argument, ask advice at Abel.' For we always give wise counsel" (2 Samuel 20:18).

With the accession of Solomon came the golden age of wisdom. The wisdom movement had spread through Egypt and Mesopotamia and become a cultural phenomenon of the ancient world. In the courts of the monarch the wise person was held in high esteem. Preeminent among these was Solomon. Of Solomon's wisdom it was said, "His wisdom excelled that of any of the wise men of the East including those of Egypt. He was wiser than Ethan the Ezrahite and Herman, Calcol, and Darda, the sons of Mahol; and he was famous among all the surrounding nations" (1 Kings 4:30–31). The inference is that wisdom was highly prized in the civilizations of that day, but Solomon excelled all the others.

Although we know Solomon asked God for wisdom, it was a crisis in family relationships that established his reputation as a wise man. The story is well known. Two women had appeared before the king and presented their cases. Both had babies. One accidently rolled over on her infant and smothered him. She exchanged the dead child for the other woman's baby, leaving her to awaken in the morning with the dead child beside her. She knew the dead child was not hers and confronted her friend, but the first mother denied the accusation that she had switched the children.

As every Sundy School child knows, Solomon made a quick decision and called for a sword—then gave the order, "Cut the living child in two and give half to each of the women."

One woman said, "All right, it will be neither yours nor mine—divide it between us."

The other's response, "Oh, no sir! Give her the child—don't kill him."

The king rendered his verdict, "Give the baby to the woman who wants him to live, for she is the mother."

Several interesting lines of thought emerge from this incident. These women were apparently prostitutes. How come the king was counseling such a case? It is possible some of the courtiers wishing to provoke some expression of wisdom might have presented the case in the royal court. Another fascinating possibility is that the king may have had a type of "open house," where petitioners brought their pleas to his residence. Another possibility is that on occasions he sat at the gates of the city with the wise men. The incident preeminently indicated Solomon's wise insight into human nature, particularly with regard to motherhood.

The setting for much of the counseling in those days was quite different from that of a modern counselor's office with its appointments schedule, waiting room replete with well-thumbed and outdated magazines, subdued lighting, psychological testing, chatty receptionists, and properly aloof psychotherapists. Those pioneer counselors plied their professions in locations as divergent as the royal court, private homes within the community, and at the ever-popular gate of the city.

The city gate had far more significance in an ancient Eastern city than it has today. Since the city lay within a protective wall, the gate was the place everybody passed when entering or leaving the metropolis. Busy commerce was carried on there and in some cities there were special gates for individual commodities, such as a fish gate, sheep gate, and a horse gate (Neh. 3:1,3,28). The legal tribunals of that day were located at the gate as judges met to deliberate and deliver their verdicts, and on occasions the king held court at the gate.

The gate was also the place for counselors to gather. Wise men sitting at the gates looked on a passing procession of humanity, the affluent balancing on slouching camels, farmers astride donkeys, the poor afoot, children laughing and chasing, yapping dogs. Amid the swirl of humanity and animal life with a hot wind blowing dust, aromas to offend sensitive nostrils, flies to irritate and annoy—some type of counseling took place as troubled people sought out and sat with the men known as "the wise."

The content of the wise men's counsel was probably much as it is today, and it obviously included a lot about home and family life. The one dramatic incident of Solomon's rendering his judgment about the baby tremendously enhanced his reputation. "Word of the king's decision spread throughout the entire nation, and all the people were awed as they realized the great wisdom God had given him" (1 Kings 3:28). In a real sense Solomon's reputation came from an experience in family counseling. Although there were many types of counseling, the book of Proverbs indicates family problems were at the fore.

From the work of these wise men in that ancient day came much of the material contained in the book of Proverbs. Apparently one of the most-honored methods of counseling was to quote a proverb, a short, easily remembered statement, that could be used in making a decision about the crisis situation an individual faced. This method is not as mechanical as some people might imagine. As we will note in Chapter 2, most counseling groups have some type of slogans or aphorisms which the counselor freely quotes in his discussion with his client.

So many of these wise sayings preserved in Proverbs are concerned with home and family life that it has been sometimes referred to as "the marriage and family counselor's handbook." It is especially appropriate that we should turn to this book for help with the problems that face us in our own day and age.

On the fourth of July, 1976, while Americans were celebrating the 200th anniversary of their independence, an Israeli raiding party flying a fleet of four gigantic Hercules transport planes swept through the darkness, low across Lake Victoria, to land at the Entebbe, Uganda, airport to free the hostages being held in the old terminal building. A scant ninety minutes after landing, the planes took off carrying the joyful hostages back to their Israeli home.

Included in that group of hostages was the Davidson family, Uzi and Sarah, father and mother, and their two sons, Ron and Benny. In the midst of all the dangers and tension of those days they spent locked up in the terminal building, the family found a new sense of unity. Mrs. Davidson wrote in her diary about an agreement she and her husband had concluded, "We told the boys, 'We won't die. We'll get back to Israel. We'll be together all the time.'" Then came the dramatic rescue as soldiers descended out of heaven. As Sarah described her experience, ". . . a soldier leaped toward me with Hebrew on his tongue. I felt goosepimples." [1]

In a day when we are in the midst of what *Reader's Digest* has called "The War on the Family," many authorities in the field are rightly concerned about the family's future.

In much the same way as the rescuers swept in to save a family, greeting them in Hebrew, so the wisdom of the Hebrews may be of the utmost significance in helping beleagured families today.

2

THE SHAPE OF PROVERBIAL WISDOM

Love wisdom like a sweetheart: make her a beloved member of your family.   Proverbs 7:4

In a day when women had been relegated to the functions of mothering and housekeeping, Eleanor of Aquitaine struck a blow for a new status of womanhood. As the queen of France in the twelfth century she went on the Second Crusade to Palestine with her husband, King Philip of France. Perhaps the first woman ever to attempt such a feat, she may have come on too strongly for the monkish Philip who finally separated from her in what became known as "the greatest divorce in history."

Eleanor's second venture into marriage was with Henry, the Duke of Normandy, known as Plantagenant, because of the sprig of broom he wore in his bonnet. By a strange set of circumstances Henry fell heir to the British throne, thus making Eleanor the Queen of England—queen for the second time in her life. This unusual woman had an aura of romance about her. Wife of two kings, she was the mother of two more in the persons of her sons, Richard the Lion-hearted and John Lackland. Two of her daughters ascended to the throne—Eleanor of Castile and Joanne, Queen of Sicily. She launched herself on many exploits, including heroic efforts to ransom her son, Richard the Lion-hearted, after he'd been captured and imprisoned in Austria. She not only pressured the English people to raise the high ransom but undertook the journey across the continent to negotiate his release.

Eleanor's place in history, however, is not assured by her heroic exploits, but rather by the romantic interlude of the years she spent at Poitiers where she popularized the notions of gentleness, courtesy and compassion. Living in her castle, she gathered around her a court thronging with poets, philosophers, clerics, and knights. Her daughter (by the king of France) Marie, the Countess of Champagne who had been wooed by Henry before he took her mother to wife, joined forces with Eleanor, and by their united efforts they developed the Court of Love. The Court of Love pondered the problems faced by people in their love life. Some historians feel these women by their work may have codified and immortalized the concept of romantic love. Eleanor is known by many titles including, "the greatest French woman of history" and "the medieval Emily Post," the latter term indicating her influence in laying down principles of behavior between the sexes.

Eleanor's feats were all the more remarkable because she was a woman—a woman who left her indelible imprint on history. Strange though it may seem, the book of Proverbs has a similar idea. Wisdom is personified as a woman, "Wisdom shouts in the streets for a hearing. *She* calls out to the crowds" (Proverbs 1:20–21). "Say unto wisdom, 'Thou art my sister'" (Proverbs 7:4). This personified wisdom is influencing people as they utilize the resources preserved in the book of Proverbs. A greater than Eleanor of Aquitaine is here and a study of this whole idea of wisdom can provide us with a good basis for examining proverbial family life. Through it we may learn to, "Love wisdom like a sweetheart. Make her a beloved member of your family" (Proverbs 7:4).

THE FIVE FACES OF WISDOM

Studying wisdom is like examining the makeup of a rainbow in which there are a number of component colors, each of which shades into the other. The five components of wisdom are seen in five words used in the opening passage of the book.

1. *Self-discipline*—"He wrote them to teach his people how to live" (Proverbs 1:2a).

The Hebrew word translated "how to live" has behind it the idea of a discipline that takes hard work, effort, and energy to gain its objective. The book of Proverbs carries a recurring message lauding the virtues of hard work and self-control and pours out scorn on the self-indulgent lazy person. In the King James Version he is personified as "the sluggard," a strange character who is hinged to his bed (26:14). Four aspects of the lazy person are shown:

(1) *He can't get started.* Asked, "When will you wake up?" His answer, "Let me sleep a little longer" (Proverbs 6:9–10).

(2) *He will not finish things.* When at last he manages to start a task he fails to follow through. "A lazy man won't even dress the game he gets while hunting but the diligent man makes good use of everything he finds" (Proverbs 12:27).

(3) *He is irresponsible.* The lazy man offers excuses for his behavior rather than to face the reality of it. "The lazy man is full of excuses. 'I can't go to work!' he says. 'If I go outside I might meet a lion in the street and be killed!'" (Proverbs 22:12).

(4) *Life is unsatisfactory.* "A lazy fellow has trouble all through life" (Proverbs 15:19). "Idle hands are the devil's workshop" (Proverbs 16:27).

For each of these there is an antithesis which calls

for energy, enthusiasm, and self-discipline. Referring to the feats of the Roman soldiers who, in addition to their practiced skill with arms, took spade and pick ax to construct the fortifications of their camps, Gibbon says, "Active valor may often be the present of nature: but such patient diligence can be the fruit only of habit and discipline." Acquiring wisdom commences with the self-discipline of mastering significant life-changing concepts.

2. *Understanding*—"To perceive the words of understanding" (KJV). "How to act in every circumstance" (TLB). [Proverbs 1:2b]

The word used here in Proverbs 1:2b is *bina,* translated in the King James Version, "understanding." Coupled with the idea of understanding is the concept of insight, seeing what lies behind the obvious.

This is the word Solomon used in his response to God. The Almighty asked him, "Ask what I shall give to thee." Among other things Solomon requested, "Give me an understanding mind so I can govern your people and know the difference between what is right and what is wrong" (1 KINGS 3:9). "The Serenity Prayer" has a similar idea.

> *Lord, Grant me the serenity to*
> *accept the things I cannot change,*
> *The courage to change the things*
> *that I can,*
> *And the wisdom to know the difference.*

It is small wonder that an organization like Alcoholics Anonymous has taken over "The Serenity Prayer" and made it their own property. The capacity to make moral choices and to know the difference will always be of importance.

3. *Wise Relationships* "He wanted them to understand" (Proverbs 1:3a).

The Hebrew word is translated "instruction" (KJV) and "understanding" (TLB). However, the idea behind it is to be able to see relationships.

The concept of wise relationships was displayed by Abigail, the wife of the churlish and arrogant Nabal. At the time when David and his band of free booters were still outlaws and seeking to gain possession of the kingdom, an emissary of David's group approached Nabal, a wealthy and affluent man, to suggest he might make a donation to their cause. Nabal gave the messengers a cold and insulting reception. They returned to report the matter to David. When he received the news, David took umbrage and planned to attack the insolent Nabal. But Nabal's wife Abigail, described as a beautiful, intelligent woman, took food and presents which she presented to David and his men. She accepted the blame for what had happened, and David, impressed by her, commended her good sense and called off the attack.

As a footnote we might notice that when Nabal later died David took the beautiful Abigail for his wife. It is possible that he later told his son, Solomon, about Abigail and the way in which she had been able to establish good relationships. The capacity to be tactful, patch up broken relationships, and establish relationships is a function of wisdom.

4. *Planning.* "I want to warn the young men about some problems they will face" (Proverbs 1:4b).

Many modern counselors lay a heavy emphasis on the concept of maturity. Planning is one of the frequently mentioned aspects of maturity. Dr. C. Buhler and her associates did a study of two hundred life histories of outstanding people. They concluded that successful people had ordered lives which steered toward selected goals, and that each person had something to live for. Another study of would-be suicides indicated they felt their lives had become intolerable because they had nothing to aim for, no goal to seek.

Proverbs makes a series of statements about planning.

"A wise man thinks ahead; a fool doesn't, and even brags about it" (*13:16*).

"The wise man looks ahead. The fool attempts to fool himself and won't face facts" (*14:9*).

"A prudent man foresees the difficulties ahead and prepares for them; the simpleton goes blindly on and suffers the consequences" (*22:3*).

"A sensible man watches for problems ahead and prepares to meet them. The simpleton never looks, and suffers the consequences" (*27:12*).

Gordon Allport once stated, "Every mature personality may be said to travel towards a destination, selected in advance, or to related ports in succession." In the light of this personality theorist's statement, Proverbs sounds strangely modern for, when Solomon states the purpose of writing, he says, "I want to warn young men about some problems they will face" (Proverbs 1:4). A study of wisdom as set out in Proverbs will hopefully lead us into some planning activities.

5. *Learning.* "A wise man will hear and increase learning; and a man of understanding shall attain unto wise counsels" (1:5, KJV).

From the Hebrew two emphases emerge concerning teaching and learning. First is an expected nautical metaphor as one word has two roots, "to bind" and "a rope." Unlike the British, for example, who because of their island home were always interested in the sea, the Hebrews paid scant attention to the Mediterranean lying on their western border. For them the heaving seas often represented mystery and turmoil—consequently navigation was a complicated task. Elliott translates the Hebrew word represented in the King James Version as "wise counsel" with the phrase "arts of seamanship." Wise counsel will be as difficult to master as will be the art of navigating a ship through the sea.

A second emphasis is the word "learning" which is derived from a word meaning "to take." Especially among the ancients, who looked upon some people as authorities and teachers seen as special individuals with ideas to be passed on to their students, teaching was a process of giving and taking. For the serious seeker after wisdom there must be an active process of constantly taking.

In TLB the emphasis on teaching and learning becomes even clearer, "I want those who are really wise to become wiser, and become leaders by exploring these nuggets of truth" (1:5). Wisdom is a constant, growing, expanding experience. We must constantly recognize the limitations of our knowledge. An encyclopedia had a little verse inside of it which read, "All things I thought I knew but now confess, the more I know, I know, I know the less." The attitude of the wise person is to be continually learning more.

THE LANGUAGE OF WISDOM

How does a world leader get his message across while visiting the nation he sees as his own country's most deadly enemy? By long speeches and short proverbs.

When Nikita Khrushchev, the premier of the USSR, visited the United States, he delivered lengthy discourses, on one occasion at least two hours in duration. But he spiced up these long harangues with a series of proverbs.

In many ways proverbs were the secret of his success in public relations. One news magazine covering his visit described the premier as, "A man with a proverb for any occasion." Some of these were very apt. Warning against delays: "Too choosy a bride will wait too long and find herself an old maid," and "He who comes too late must be content with a picked bone." The value of touring: "To see it once is better than to read a hundred times." On the collapse of Communism: "Those who expect this will have to wait until Easter falls on Tuesday." About allowing political opposition in Russia: "That would be like voluntarily letting someone put a flea in your shirt."

In many of his mannerisms, the premier, who removed his shoe and banged on the table during a United Nations meeting, and looked into the face of Americans on television and said, "We will bury you," was uncouth and rude, but he charmed many people who saw him as a personable, affable, friendly man, and this image came in large measure from the homespun proverbs he used.

Benjamin Franklin impressed himself on American life not only because of his work as a statesman and an ambassador and a founding father, but in a large measure by the proverbs he collected in what is known as *Poor Richard's Almanac*. Some of his proverbs have become an integral part of our culture, "God helps those who help themselves," "A good wife and health are a man's best wealth," "Constant dropping wears away stones," "For want of a nail the shoe was lost, for want of a shoe the horse was lost, and for want of a horse the rider was lost," "When the well's dry they know the worth of water."

The practice of using proverbs is as old as speech itself, and Aristotle, the famous philosopher, is sometimes claimed to be the first person to put together a collection of proverbs, but the Bible preceded him with its extraordinary compendium known as the book of Proverbs. Other proverbs appear in various parts of the Old Testament. In the New Testament, Jesus used proverbs to convey his ideas. On the occasion of his first public appearance he referred to the proverb, "Physician, heal thyself." Facing opposition he quoted, "A prophet is not without honor save in his own country." At the well of Sychar he stated, "Herein is the saying true 'one soweth and another reapeth.' "

What is a proverb? Even though we use proverbs freely and can apply them to many situations, few of us can actually define a proverb.

Although I am vividly aware of three proverbs: "Fools rush in where angels fear to tread," "Wise men make proverbs, and fools repeat them," and the biblical statement, "In the mouth of a fool a proverb becomes as useless as a paralyzed leg," I will try to come up with a few rudimentary ideas about proverbs.

Some of the best definitions of proverbs are:

"A short pithy statement in common recognized use."

"A wise saying or precept, a didactic saying."

"The wit of one and the wisdom of many."

"A common and pithy expression which embodies some moral precept or admitted truth."

The book of Proverbs is a collection of these "nuggets of truth" and early makes a statement, "To understand a proverb and a figure, the words of the wise, and their dark sayings . . ." (1:6, KJV).

There seem to be two basic ideas here. "Proverb" and "words of the wise" are apparently synonyms and then an elaboration that indicates two aspects of the proverb; the obvious, "a figure" and the hidden "dark sayings," the latter being the word translated "riddle" in other places as in Samson's riddle (Judges 14:13–13). This aspect of a proverb indicates the way in which the individual was to draw on experience, "catch on" as to what is the real meaning.

The Hebrew word translated "proverbs" has the basic idea of comparison, but it takes a number of different forms in the way in which it is used.

(1) A simple comparison

"A beautiful woman lacking discretion and modesty is like a fine gold ring in a pig's snout" (11:22).

(2) *The idea in the first line is repeated in the second.*

"If you want people to like you, forgive them when they wrong you. Remembering wrongs can break up friendships" (17:19).

(3) *A second line may illustrate the first by presenting a contrast to it.*

A wise son maketh a glad father: but a foolish son is the heaviness of his mother" (10:1, KJV).

(4) *Staircase parallelism. The second line appears to complete or fulfill what is promised in the first.*

"Teach a child to choose the right path, and when he is older he will remain upon it" (22:6).

(5) *Two distinct truths with little relationship may be presented.*

"A cloak of hatred are lying lips, and he that spreadeth a slander is a fool" (10:18).

(6) *Sometimes it may be just a simple statement.*

"Listen and grow wise" (4:1).

(7) *The twist. The statement finishes with an unusual idea.*

"Some rich people are poor, and some poor people have great wealth! Being kidnapped and held for ransom never worries the poor man!" (13:7–8).

"A lazy man sleeps soundly—and goes hungry!" (19:15).

These short, pithy, easily remembered statements are typical of some of the techniques used in the more informal type of counseling today. The word slogan originally meant a battle cry, and most popular movements seeking to influence others make use of slogans to carry their ideas. So in political circles "The Communist Manifesto" reminds its followers, "The workers have nothing to lose but their chains," and in an American presidential campaign a similar emphasis has been seen in the slogan, "All the way with LBJ."

The so-called self-help groups have majored on slogans and epigrams. Any Alcoholics Anonymous meeting place is adorned with sayings to give its members easy guidelines for decision-making: "Easy does it," "A day at a time," "But for the grace of God," "Think, think, think." Reminding them of their technique is, "We carry the message, not the alcoholic." "The Twelve Steps" and "The Twelve Traditions" have become "inspired words," giving an easily remembered philosophy for A.A. groups.

Integrity Therapy has its list of slogans borrowed from a number of sources. It has a saying to fit many of the peculiar situations arising in this therapy. On the action emphasis, "It is much easier to act yourself into a new way of feeling than to feel yourself into a new way of acting." About confession, "We do not confess for somebody else." Concerning the fellowship of the group, "We are all strugglers together in the sea of life." The power of the group, "We alone can do it, but we cannot do it alone." On putting oneself in a dangerous position, "Don't sit near the fire if your head is made of butter."

The summary of an idea into a catchy phrase gives the group member a little piece of truth which he can easily grasp and tuck away in a mental recess, close at hand and ready to be used in the moment of need. It is a modern example of the use of the proverbs as seen in Solomon's day.

WISDOM AND THE FAMILY

The family as an organization is mentioned only about five times in the book of Proverbs, but the spirit and ideals of family life, like some recurring motif in a beautiful piece of music, leap out from every page of the book. In the midst of a polygamous age, Solomon presents the alternative of fidelity to a partner with a family to be reared in the fear and admonition of the Lord. Solomon, a product of a polygamous home, was vividly aware of all the problems of family life that arose in such a setting.

Family solidarity is a constant note in Proverbs. The crowning argument against adultery is the integrity of family, "Why share your children with those outside your home?" (5:17). This precious family unit must be kept intact, and an adulterous relationship may cause the vital family life to be diluted. The modern statement of a person considering breaking up a family unit and saying, "It would be foolish for us to stay together just for the sake of the family," would find no place in Solomon's thought. All conduct is to be considered in terms of what it would do to the family.

Turning from sins of the flesh to deal with sins of the spirit, the book of Proverbs is equally emphatic and takes on a strangely modern note as it warns about the dangers of resentment. The word resent comes from two Latin words literally meaning to "feel back," and a resentful family is one which is constantly feeling back to events of the past. The foolish man doesn't worry about upsetting his family, spoiling their spirit, and making them angry. This attitude means that he will not only destroy his family, but he will bring ruin upon himself and might even lose his own precious freedom. "The fool who provokes his family to anger and resentment will finally have nothing worthwhile left. He shall be the servant of a wiser man" (11:29).

It has sometimes been said that a modern vow might be changed to "till debt us do part" in consideration of the financial problems that come to many families today. Thus the book of Proverbs spends a lot of time talking about finances as we will notice in a later chapter. Many troubles come to a family that lives beyond its means. In Solomon's day, this style of life was referred to as "dishonest money," and to this day dishonest money brings its problems. As Solomon stated, "Dishonest money brings grief to all the family" (15:17).

The book of Proverbs opens with a series of chapters of admonition from a father to his son and ends with a long chapter on the ideal wife. The chapters in between are sprinkled with proverbs about family life and giving counsel about the temptations of the young, problems of family finance, communication difficulties, the danger of jealousy and temper, the importance of disciplining the children, perspectives on the aging process, and the importance of fidelity in marriage.

It may seem at first blush that problems of polygamy have little to do with an age in which the polygamy of Solomon's day is a violation of the law of the land. We may have to remind ourselves that we are actually faced with a new polygamy in our day. Today's divorce laws have given rise to what could be called "serial polygamy." Men still have a number of wives, but they have them successively; nevertheless the practice is just as disruptive of family life as it was in Solomon's day.

There is only one sense in which there can be a second woman in the proverbial family. Solomon states it quite clearly, "Love wisdom like a sweetheart; make her a beloved member of your family" (7:4).

PROVERBIAL TEACHINGS
ABOUT WISDOM

Proverbs 1:7	*Proverbs 9:11–12*
Proverbs 1:20–33	*Proberbs 10:8*
Proverbs 2:1–5	*Proverbs 13:2*
Proverbs 2:6–15	*Proverbs 14:6*
Proverbs 2:16–19	*Proverbs 14:24*
Proverbs 3:13–15	*Proverbs 14:33*
Proverbs 3:16–17	*Proverbs 15:33*
Proverbs 3:18	*Proverbs 16:16*
Proverbs 3:19–20	*Proverbs 16:22*
Proverbs 3:21–26	*Proverbs 17:24*
Proverbs 4:1–6	*Proverbs 19:8*
Proverbs 4:7–10	*Proverbs 21:22*
Proverbs 7:4	*Proverbs 24:5*
Proverbs 8:1–21	*Proverbs 24:13–14*
Proverbs 9:1–6	*Proverbs 28:16*
Proverbs 9:7–9	*Proverbs 29:15*
Proverbs 9:10	*Proverbs 30:24–27*

3

PROVERBIAL RELATIONSHIPS BETWEEN HUSBAND AND WIFE

My son, keep thy father's commandment, and forsake not the law of thy mother.   *Proverbs 6:20, KJV*

Solomon grew up in a polygamous home. Aware his own mother, Bathsheba, was a favorite wife of David, he noted how she worked on her husband to make sure *her* son would be David's sucessor to the throne. He watched the behind-the-scenes power struggles, as various wives tried to improve the lot of their children, and he grew to hate the bickering of contending wives. He noted, too, the bitterness of many of these frustrated women and how they became quarrelsome nags as the years passed.

We generally think of Solomon as the great builder who constructed the famous Temple and residence for himself. But he built other things. He built an idea about the family in general and husband-and-wife relationships in particular. We are going to consider some of his ideas about husband/wife relationships which can be of help to us today.

FOR BETTER OR FOR WORSE

Proverbs takes a realistic view of life, and this is never more clearly seen than in the way it portrays women. Women have two potentialities in a marriage relationship,

"A virtuous woman is a crown to her husband, but she that maketh ashamed is as rottenness in his bones" (12:4, KJV). The two types of women—the one who is "a crown to her husband," and the other stated to be "as rottenness in his bones"—are specifically described. This way of doing it has a strangely modern sound. Behavioral psychologists indicate the futility of hanging labels upon people, insisting that we "pinpoint" or describe specific behavior. And Proverbs does this. The woman who is a "crown to her husband" is described in considerable detail in the 31st chapter of the book. Later on we will discuss this woman's virtues. With its usual candor this same book describes the "rottenness-in-his-bones" type of wife, and there seem to be three major characteristics about these women who are complainers and crank naggers.

COMPLAINING

"You can no more stop her complaints than you can stop the wind" (27:16).
Complaining is a chronic ailment with some people. The word "complaint" itself means a sickness, and a manifestation of this sickness is seen in a series of complaints. This sickness can hide under a number of disguises. In one type of group therapy, newcomers are given an opportunity to "become open" and tell about their situations. They are urged to discuss their failures, but all too frequently it becomes a lament about what people have done to them. When this happens, perceptive group members will quickly zero in on the recital and say, "That is not confessing—it is complaining." Complaining is a futile procedure, the main outcome being to allow the subject to have a bath of self-pity, constantly feeling sorry for himself.

The Bible sees it another way. Paul in his magnificant hymn to love (1 Cor. 13) expresses it, "Love believeth all things, hopeth all things, endureth all things." *Agape*

love, then, is the complete opposite of a complaining attitude.

CRANKINESS

"It is better to dwell in a corner of the housetop,
than with a brawling woman in a wide house" (21:9, KJV).
Cranky, quarrelsome people are generally lonely individuals, because others do not want to be around them.
They have a bad attitude. The word attitude comes from
the word "aptitude" and has behind it the idea of a posture.
So an attitude is a posture of the mind. The cranky person
has a certain posture; they are ready to react negatively at
any opportunity. One of the most interesting creatures of
the sea world is the spiny sea urchin. It is covered with
hundreds of shiny spines. Knowledgeable people keep away
from the spiny sea urchin because to touch it is to be
pricked. Cranky people are like that. They are so prickly
we soon learn to avoid them.

All of this is in contrast with what life should be in
the home where wisdom reigns. The New Testament
equivalent of the Wisdom Literature, the Epistle of James,
speaks to this subject, "The wisdom that comes from heaven
—is full of quiet gentleness" (James 3:17). All through the
book of Proverbs there is constant use of the Hebrew word
hesed meaning kindness. Some ten times over the writers
tell of all the things kindness accomplishes. Among other
things, kindness brings its own rewards (11:17), kindness
begets kindness (14:22), kindness makes a man attractive
(19:22), and preeminently, kindness brings a sense of
unity to a family (31:26). The family, then, is to be unified by a kind spirit wherein if any member has a bad attitude it affects the family harmony. But it is particularly important that the wife should adorn the home with a quiet
and kind spirit.

NAGGING

"A nagging wife annoys like constant dripping" (19:13).

The Romans used to say, "Repetition is the mother of learning," and more modern sages have expressed the same concept as "repetition breeds retention." Many a wife and mother trying to get an idea across to her husband or children has intuitively used the principle with far less than satisfactory results. The person who launches a verbal bombardment has some vague notion that the quantity of speech will overwhelm and convince her family, but it is seldom effective.

One peculiarity of the United States Senate is the phenomenon of the filibuster. Utilizing this legislative tactic, a senator or group of senators opposed to a bill under consideration talk on *ad infinitum* until weary colleagues despair and drop the offensive legislation. There's a great deal of talk—Senator Strom Thurmond once discoursed for 24 hours and 18 minutes, and a team effort aimed at the Civil Rights Bill of 1964 created a record by holding the floor for seventy-two days. Much of this talk was frequently completely irrelevant. When Senator Huey Long was holding the floor, he included the recipe for "potlikker," and some filibusters have resorted to such tactics as reading telephone directories, the *World Almanac*, a treatise on butterfly anatomy, and *Aesop's Fables*. There is much speech, many words, but these are obstructionist tactics, and there's no real attempt at communication.

Beethoven is credited with saying a musical composition must have two elements—familiarity and uniqueness. The same principle applies to most communicable material. Information completely new and unfamiliar can frustrate the listener and fail to catch his interest. People love the familiar. Consider the child requesting the oft-repeated story and delightedly joining in at known climactic points or the adult responding to a well-known tune.

But let a message be too familiar, and it becomes boring and calls for responses, "I kicked the bottom out of my cradle when I first heard that," or a derisive gesture indicating the information is old and bewhiskered.

Which leads us to the communication technique known as "nagging." Nagging fails as a communication technique because of the familiarity of the material.

The word nag has been defined as, "To torment by persistent fault-finding, complaints, or importunities," and *The Oxford Dictionary* further adds to the definition and says it means "to gnaw, bite, nibble." Many families do not enjoy this torment and become defensive and fight back. In one family whenever mother introduced certain ideas the whole family would commence to sing, "Tell Me the Old, Old Story." So mother's good intentions were continually frustrated. Strangely enough, she often felt she was being martyred. In that sense she gained something out of the experience but achieved nothing as far as communications were concerned.

If you are tempted to nag, here are some hints about how you can avoid this pitfall.

(1) Don't make a predictable response.

(2) Remember, no matter what satisfaction it gives you, nagging has a negative influence on your family, so you've accomplished nothing.

(3) Be subtle. Get your idea across in as many different ways as you can.

(4) Acknowledge you don't know everything, and you could just be wrong.

(5) Build the logic of your ideas so the family will be able to reach some conclusions of their own.

(6) Don't gloat over it when the logic of it proves you to be correct.

There is a final antidote to the nagging problem as Solomon sees it: "Love forgets mistakes; nagging about them parts the best of friends" (17:9).

MAN'S BEST FRIEND

Is the dog really man's best friend? I don't suppose it ever hit me so forcibly as when I met a handsome couple in their late thirties. At the man's side sat General, an enormous, seeing-eye dog who deftly guided his recently blinded master as they moved around. The man's well-cut suit, coordinated accessories, carefully styled hair, highly polished shoes all gave evidence of his wife's attention and loving care. But wherever the man moved, all attention was on the dog. The wife, a beautiful former beauty queen, was the third member of the party, and I wondered within myself as to what she really inwardly thought of General, "man's best friend," when *she* so obviously was her husband's very best friend and without her, his life would have been immeasurably complicated.

Tony Randall, known for his game-show image as an egghead and consummate acting ability in TV sitcoms, has revealed his uneasiness about his role. "I must say I'm funny, and it annoys me—I've always wanted to be a romantic." When it comes to marriage, he is a romantic and more. Married for thirty-five years he says, "My wife is my best friend," thus confirming the verdict of a writer on the role of a wife. Morton Hunt in his *Natural History of Love* quotes what has been called the cruelest epigram in Grecian literature, "There are only two happy days in a married man's life, the day he takes his bride to bed and the day he lays her in the grave." He claims that wives have meant different things to their husbands—lovers, mothers of children, housekeepers—but says the modern idea of a wife is that she is a husband's *friend,* and goes on to note the idea would have ". . . thoroughly offended St. Paul, bewildered Tristan and amused Don Juan."

Perhaps Hunt should have read the book of Proverbs where the writer says a lot about friends and remarks that a breakup of a marriage comes because of unfaithfulness, "These girls have abandoned their husbands and flounted the laws of God" (2:17). The Hebrew word in this passage is one used of the closest of friends: ". . . gossip separates the best of friends" (16:28). "Love forgets mistakes, nagging about them parts the best of friends" (17:9). Contrast this view of a wife as a friend with the common, pagan attitude towards women who at their worst are seen as chattels; at their best, bearers of children. This wife in Proverbs is to be the man's *friend,* an idea that is developed in Proverbs 31 where the picture of the ideal woman is presented; she is seen as a partner involved in a wide variety of enterprises in the course of which she "satisfied his needs," and he "praises her."

In our English language we use a single word for love, but the Greeks had three available. The word *eros* referred to romantic, emotional, sexual love; *philia,* the companionate, intellectual love; and *agape,* the giving or volitional type of love. The love referred to in this statement is akin to *philia,* the love of friends.

It may be a commentary on our present-day culture that many people cannot comprehend the importance of friendship. If two people of the same sex become close friends it isn't long before someone is insinuating there might be something wrong, and the implications of homosexuality are made. An examination of some contrasts between friendship and romantic love will help us to understand the importance of friendship in an age when romantic love reigns supreme.

Romantic love is fostered by differences. Lovers in the unreal aspects of their infatuation will confess, "We don't really like each other, but we fell in love." The very differences of background and interests were actually a factor in fostering the romantic episode, making the unusual partner attractive. When the emotional impact subsided, the lovers found themselves either antagonists in a protracted conflict or strangers living in two different and isolated worlds. Friendship on the other hand lacks the *eros* emotional, sexual reinforcement, but depends on an affinity of interests which cements and holds the friends together.

Friends and romantic lovers face in different directions. Romantic lovers are face to face with the loved object absorbing all the lover's attention. To talk to a young woman in the throes of romantic love is to feel akin to a midnight visitor in a haunted castle, with the ghost constantly flitting backward and forward, and dogging every footstep. Discuss the weather, and it reminds Susan of the perfect day when Stanley first held her hand. Talk of a trip to New Mexico, and she recalls that if she had not taken her vacation in Florida she would never have met him. Mention an alumni meeting, and Susan launches into a long discourse on Stanley's academic prowess. It matters not where conversation starts—it all leads directly back to Stanley. In contrast to the romantic lovers' concentration on each other, friends are in an entirely different posture, side by side, looking in the same direction. They are bound together by mutual interests.

Romantic lovers build up a fanciful image of their beloved in which the beloved is idealized with faults overlooked. It is not unusual for a girl to describe her boyfriend, "He's all that I ever hoped a man might be," an evaluation generally out of relationship with reality. Friends on the other hand know only too well the shortcomings of each other, and there is no necessity to avoid these, for they are an integral part of one's distinctive personality. As Martin Luther bade the painter do his portrait, "warts and all," so a friend is cognizant of the blemishes and accepts them. The superiority of the love object so often seen in romantic love is unnecessary in friendship where the friend can be accepted as equal, inferior or superior, without in any way spoiling the friendship.

Possibly the most outstanding difference between romantic love and friendship is that eros *love is between just two people.* They generally have the attitude, "How can we get away from these people and be by ourselves?" Even in company they lose sight of the others. Friendship, on the other hand, can involve any number; in fact, the greater the number it involves, the more satisfactory it is likely to become. And jealousy which has been seen as the nurse of romantic love has no part in friendship. We are happy to share a friend and proud of the opportunities which come his way.

Friendship is beneficial to the community. Many of the greatest movements to help society have commenced with a few like-minded people who gathered themselves into some form of association and committed themselves to a common objective. Their loyalty to the objective and to each other made an impact. *Philia* love will clearly be a significant factor within the family as concern spreads to a group of people within the interacting family system.

AN UNLIMITED PARTNERSHIP

It might be imagined that Proverbs, deeply embedded in the Old Testament, would be the last place we would expect to find the concept of a husband/wife partnership. Yet it is surely here. The message constantly comes through as is seen in the following typical verses.

> *My son, hear the instruction of thy* father, *and forsake not the law of thy* mother: *For they shall be an ornament of grace unto thy head, and chains about thy neck* (1:8–9, KJV).

My son, keep thy father's *commandment, and forsake*
not the law of thy mother *(6:20, KJV).*

Her husband can trust her, and she will richly satisfy
his needs (31:11).

All of this is not new. In his commentary (on the
Genesis account of God's taking a rib from Adam's side to
create a wife for him), one person remarked "the woman
was made of a rib out of the side of Adam; not made out of
his head to rule over him nor out of his feet to be trampled
upon by him; but out of his side to be equal with him, under
his arm to be protected, and near his heart to be loved."

The way men feel about their wives is often indicated by the names they use when speaking about them.
Martin Luther, the reformer, steeped in the Scriptures,
thought of his wife as God's special creation for him and
referred to Katie as "my rib." John Wesley, planning to
marry Grace Murray, was attracted to her as he watched
the way she organized his societies and effectively worked
with people as his associate. So he called her "my right
hand." David Livingstone in Africa, where a wagon was
the main vehicle for transportation which enabled him to
move through the unexplored hinterland, heard people refer to his wife Mary as the "queen of the wagon." He came
to speak about her as "the main spoke of my wheel." My
rib, my right hand, the main spoke in my wheel—all these
names indicate what an integral part their wives played as
partners in their enterprises.

The partnership set up by a husband and a wife is
one of two independent personalities who have each learned
to retain personal individuality, while at the same time relating to each other. Amid all the sorry offerings on television there suddenly appeared a remarkable program,
"The Incredible Machine." A presentation from the National Geographic Society, it showed how a human body—
two-thirds water, the rest nitrogen and carbon calcium, and

a myriad of other chemicals worth only about five dollars at today's inflated prices—is nevertheless amazing in its functioning. Nowhere was this more dramatically indicated then in a demonstration of cells from a heart muscle which were lying in a culture dish. Each cell continues to pulsate at a distinctive, individual rhythm until the two were pushed into contact with each other. Once the edges of the cells touched, the two cells immediately abandoned their individual rhythm to beat in unison.

Husbands and wives are like this. Each has his or her own unique rhythm of life and brings something peculiar to the marriage relationship. However, in marriage the two learn to live in a distinctive, interacting rhythm.

There are two kinds of partnership. One generally referred to as a limited partnership implies that the partner has only certain agreed-upon responsibilities. By way of contrast, a full partnership means both partners share the full obligations for each other. Marriage is this kind of partnership.

PROVERBIAL RELATIONSHIPS BETWEEN HUSBAND AND WIFE

Proverbs 1:8–9	*Proverbs 6:32–33*
Proverbs 2:16	*Proverbs 12:4*
Proverbs 5:18–19	*Proverbs 14:1*
Proverbs 6:20	*Proverbs 18:22*
Proverbs 6:26	*Proverbs 19:14*
Proverbs 6:28–29	*Proverbs 31:11*

4

OLD WISDOM FOR YOUNG PEOPLE

*I want to warn young men about some problems
they will face.*   *Proverbs 1:4*

Proverbs is in some ways as up-to-date as today's newspaper. This is particularly true of that period of life we call adolescence. Historically, the scientific study of adolescence began with the work of G. Stanley Hall at the end of the last century, but Proverbs clearly indicates that the struggles of adolescents and their parents were a feature of Solomon's day. The book comes up with a series of suggestions about relating to adolescents that sound as modern as a current adolescent psychology text book.

What happens in adolescence? Children who are formerly open and communicative all too frequently become secretive and build a wall between themselves and the other members of the family. One father, bothered by the constant prattle of his preschool child commented: "Talk! Talk! Talk! Thank heavens, in a few years he'll be a teenager, and we won't be able to communicate with him!"

But when these adolescent years come, a parent faced with incommunicado teenagers may have some troubled moments. A father sitting at home and watching the technological miracle of pictures and sound beamed

millions of miles from the moon to the earth mentally contrasts this communications feat with his difficulty of getting
a message across the living room to his son, Jimmy.

In many ways the adolescent resembles a beginning
water skier. Anyone can water ski. It is one of the simplest
skills to learn. Children of five and six become competent
skiers. One man mastered the skill on the day of his
seventhy-fifth birthday. Despite all this, one simple aspect
of the process keeps many people from enjoying the sensa-
tion of skimming on the surface of the water. It is the problem of getting up and onto the surface.

Most people fail because they try too hard. Instead
of letting the boat haul them up, the would-be skier struggles to pull himself out of the water. Then wham! The skis
fly out from under him, and he topples over to disappear
below the surface. If the area of water below the surface
represents childhood, and the surface of the water, adulthood, then adolescence is the horrible period of coming up
out of the water. Like the skiing dropout, the adolescent
wants to be up on top, skimming around, enjoying all the
privileges of adulthood, but he tries too hard and often falls
flat on his face.

Some of the areas that will give him his greatest
problems are facing his own sexuality which will be discussed later, peer-group pressures, decisions about love and
marriage, and relationships with other members of the
family. We will consider each of these latter three in turn.

PEER-GROUP PRESSURES

"Don't associate with radicals. For you will go down
with them to sudden disaster, and who knows where it all
will end?" (24:21–22).
As the child grows and develops so does his idea of what
he most desires. Whereas in his early days the approval of
his parents was probably the most dominant force in his

decision-making, now as he moves away from parents towards independence, he comes under the influence of a much wider group and the adulation of other adolescents—his peers—becomes tremendously important.

In a series of fascinating studies, psychologist Harry Harlow, director of the University of Wisconsin's Primate Laboratory, tried to investigate the effects of social deprivation on monkeys. After a number of studies he concluded that the affectional bonds between the baby monkey and its mother were important but needed supplementing with peer relationships. So powerful were these peer pressures that he concluded, "Opportunity for optimal infant-infant interaction may compensate for lack of mothering."

In my own years of work with therapy groups I've concluded that the most powerful pressure for changing human personality is the "peer group." What is true for these groups working with adults is doubly true for the adolescent as he begins to make his tentative steps out of the home and family and to ally himself with that great group of people we refer to as his "peers."

Adolescence is also the period of life in which the adolescent may become very idealistic and vividly aware of the inequities and shortcomings of the society within which he lives. Apparently this happened in Solomon's day, and he worried about the young people associating with "radicals," a group of people many of us thought were the products of our own age. As young people struggle to find themselves, they naturally ask many questions and traditionally held values are reassessed. The idealistic adolescent frequently feels the need to challenge adult standards, the inequities of society, the wisdom of much of our technology, the continual pollution of our environment, the necessity of grinding, hard work, and the spirit of conformity which results in people being like peas in a pod.

An adolescent's insistence on his own individuality

and concern for many of the inequities about him have led some into the trap of using violence and destruction as a means of calling attention to the situation. Gradually the idea develops that "the end justifies the means," and this coupled with an adolescent love of adventure has had some unhappy results.

When Diana Oughton joined the radical Students for a Democratic Society in the turbulent sixties, she was motivated by the highest ideals. A member of a wealthy family, she was determined to stamp out the inequities of society. She gradually gravitated to the Weathermen, the extreme group of SDS. At first shocked by drugs, collective sex, and violence, she gradually accepted the idea that violence was the only way. With a group of friends, she moved into the Greenwich Village townhouse of a vacationing friend. While she worked on making a bomb made of dynamite surrounded by nails to act as shrapnel, it exploded and killed her. Her body was so mutilated that it took eleven days to identify her. Diana stands as a symbol of the tragic possibilities of what can happen to an idealistic youth who gets caught up with an extreme group.

However, the very spirit of idealism in adolescence can offer tremendous possibilities. As a little boy with an awl in each hand ran through his father's cobbler's shop, he tripped and fell to the floor, piercing his eyes and tragically losing his sight. Later he took an awl in hand and made marks on thick paper and thus Louis Braile gave eyes to the blind by opening up the world of literature to them. The instrument of destruction became the instrument of teaching and learning. Similarly the spirit of idealism and adventure of young people can move in two directions.

Charles Nordhoff examined many of the communal societies of the eighteenth century—then concluded they were a mutiny against society but a revolt in the best way. He went on to speculate about how a revolt against society is carried out. He concluded that the determining factor as to whether the revolutionary, "shall rebel with a bludgeon and a petroleum torch, or with a plough and a church depends on whether he has or has not faith in God." [1]

The challenge of radicalism, then, is for parents and teachers to make sure the youth is challenged with the possibility of placing his faith in God.

THE GROWTH OF LOVE

"There are three things too wonderful for me to understand—no four! How an eagle glides through the sky. How a serpent crawls upon a rock. How a ship finds its way across the heaving ocean. The growth of love between a man and a girl" (30:18–19).

Solomon was always attracted by things unusual or difficult to explain. In this foursome of wonderful things he moves from the mystery of flight in the air to reptile locomotion to navigation at sea—then progresses naturally to the marvel of the manner in which male and female grow to love each other. Apparently many knowledgeable people have conveniently overlooked this Proverb's statement, along with others in the Old Testament. Some historians claim romantic love was a formulation of Eleanor of Acquitaine's "Court of Love," overlooking such experiences as that of Jacob of whom was said, "Jacob was in love with Rachel," and who offered to work for seven years for her, as it is recorded, "So Jacob spent the next seven years working for Rachel. But they seemed to him but a few days he was so much in love." A love that caused a young man to feel that seven years of hard work was just a few days must have been very intense. In similar vein Solomon marvels at the wonder of the love between a man and a woman.

The really fascinating aspect of Solomon's statement is his emphasis on the growth aspects of a love experience. During adolescence, the stage in life in which most people are more vulnerable to a love experience, the individual is also undergoing the most dramatic period of physical growth and development. It is also the period of the hormonal surge with its concomitant emotional upheaval. Considering the growth processes, Solomon focuses on "the growth of love between a man and a woman." As part and parcel of these growth experiences the adolescent faces a group of problem decisions about love and marriage which we will examine in turn.

FALLING IN LOVE

The statement of Proverbs about the "growth of love" immediately ushers us into the presence of the idea of falling in love, as is seen in the conversation between Kathy Holt, and her sister, Pat.

"Pat, what do you think has happened to me?" Kathy Holt is on the phone with her favorite married sister whom she has called long distance (collect).

Pat: "There's no telling. But keep it brief. Roger has been complaining about all these collect calls on the phone bill."

Kathy: "Pat, I've fallen in love with the most wonderful guy in the world."

Kathy is verbalizing one of the most difficult ideas of romantic love. Falling in love is an intense, sudden, dramatic experience that overtakes its subject. It's rather like falling down a hole. You're walking down the street, the manhole beneath you gives way, and down you go. You're in a wonderful, estatic state in which you expect to stay for the rest of your days.

The Menningers are not impressed by this idea and say: "One does not 'fall' in love: one grows into love and love grows in him; and this starts not in adolescence, not in maturity, but in infancy." [2] Love is a loving, vital part of personality, and like everything else that lives, it can be

LOVE OR INFATUATION

Research has indicated the following characteristics in comparing love and infatuation. Try yourself on the scales as under by checking your point on the continuum.

INFATUATION   LOVE

Short, intense	Longer duration
Unsuitable person	Appropriate person
Parents disapprove	Parents approve
Focus on few traits	Focus total personality
Loss of ambition	Brings new energy
Boredom frequent	Joy in being together
Static relationship	Grows and develops
Disregard problems	Face problems realistically
Self-centered	Feel good about others
Guilt, insecurity	Self-confidence, trust

nourished or neglected. It can be flexible and viable. Developmental factors in personality are no more significant in any other area of life than in our thought about love.

When we "fall in love" it's a good idea to test the experience as to whether it might not be a passing infatuation, rather than a viable love experience.

GETTING TO KNOW YOU

Smitten with love, the adolescent feels he knows the person whom he loves, but if love is a growth experience it takes time to really get to know someone. Within a love relationship each partner has a tendency to put the best foot forward, but as time goes on we let down our defenses and reveal the type of person we really are. A whole group of studies has shown that the longer you know your partner, the better the prospects for a good relationship. An absolute minimum is twelve months, with many authorities indicating a two-year period is to be preferred.

Of course, it isn't time alone. Take a young couple separated by his military service overseas. They have known each other for two years, but it has been a correspondence courtship. The letters they write to each other can be altogether devoid of reality. Two people need to spend a goodly amount of time in reasonably close proximity. They should get to know each other's friends. These friends will be around for a long time. What of his or her family? The couple should visit their in-laws to be, not just on weekends. Try to stay a few weeks and find out how you feel about them.

An engagement period plays its part in preparation for marriage. Four separate researchers have found an engagement period of nine months or more was positively related to a good marriage relationship. An engagement means half in and half out of marriage. As they face the assets and liabilities of their relationship, two young people frequently do much serious thinking about how this will all work out in the future.

Faced with the evidence of the value of knowing someone for two years and an engagement of nine months, many young people say, "I don't think I can wait that long." If that's the way you feel, you may have to rethink your relationship. One of the best measures of love is that it can stand the test of time.

How Important Is Age?

If love is a growth experience, the chronological age of the partners to a projected marriage will be a vital factor in assuring the development of a good relationship.

A marriage prospect who is really a good risk will be at an age characterized by both stability and flexibility. Stability is evidenced by habits and attitudes that will guide and direct life on a well-defined course. This must be tempered by a pliability seen in the individual's capacity to change, which in turn has a relationship to age. The girl who is 18 years old has a lot of flexibility but not a great amount of stability. On the other hand the man of 40 years ought to have plenty of stability, but he may not be too flexible. So it is important that marriage be entered upon at a time when there is a happy medium between the two extremes of flexibility and stability.

Another important consideration is the "quinquennium of change." If we divide life off into five-year segments, 1–5, 5–10, 10–15, 15–20, 20–25, 25–30, 30–35, and so on, we will notice each of these five-year periods has some distinctives. Which is the period of greatest change? I personally would select the 15–20-years period which I call the "quinquennium of change."

This may be the most significant period in all of life; the adolescent's body is changing, as are his relationships with his parents, school is of a new and different type, vocational plans are in a state of flux. Just at this time, when everything is changing, it is not the moment to be making the permanent, lifelong commitment that marriage calls for.

Remember, too, that other people look different within a few years. As you grow and develop your outlook will change. Your friends and acquaintances will have the same type of alteration. The guy who looks like a knight in shining armor at age 18 may appear as a dead loss when he is 25 years old.

One review of eleven studies of the relationship between age and success in marriage suggested that early marriage is a major cause of divorce and unhappiness in marriage. Early marriage is defined as before 20 for females and before 25 for males. The conclusion—the longer marriage is delayed into the twenties and early thirties, the greater the probability of a successful relationship.

Do Opposites Attract?

"A virtuous woman is a crown to her husband: but she that maketh ashamed is as rottenness in his bones (12: 4, KJV).

One of the notions frequently found among college students is that, "Opposites attract." While there has been some speculation that people may be drawn towards each other because of "complementary needs" which each may supply in the other, the evidence is clearly on the side of what is called "homogamy"—like attracts like.

The concept of homogamy has been a "happy hunting ground" for researchers, and a great number of investigations have shown that similarity runs through all the areas of good male–female relationships. Similarity of social background, attitudes, values, and philosophy of life. As unlikely as it may seem, the homogamy principle even extends to physical characteristics including color, age, height, weight, and dress. The available studies suggest you'll probably be much happier married to someone something like yourself.

In one interesting experiment with sixty-four students, investigators gave feedback about various people the student didn't know. The investigator told about the political, educational, and religious values of the various strangers. The outcome of this experiment was: when a student was told the stranger had similar values to his own, the student felt the stranger was more intelligent, moral, and better adjusted than were the people he was told had dissimilar values. One inference drawn from this experiment was that you will experience more positive feelings, including love, when relating to people with similar values than those who do not hold such values.

Be particularly careful about moving toward a marriage relationship with someone who is altogether and completely different from you. What is attractive and entrancing now may become completely irritating in future days within marriage.

What About Attitudes of Relatives and Friends?

"Young man obey your father and mother. Tie their instructions around your finger so you won't forget. Take to heart all of their advice" (6:20–22).
In the days of Proverbs, as in many Eastern countries today, parents make the choice of the persons their children will marry. One sociologist visiting the Orient heard about this and sympathized, "Isn't it a shame that your parents should choose your future spouse instead of the way we do it in America?" The Eastern girl responded, "Do your marriages turn out better than ours?" The sociologist reluctantly admitted that our divorce rate told its own tale.

Despite all our freedom in America, the opinion of parents and friends is still important in making a marriage choice. This is not hearsay—a whole group of studies has shown the approval of parents and friends is a factor in helping to establish a good marriage relationship. If there is anything like a sizable majority of relatives and friends opposed to your marriage, you might do well to sit down and rethink the situation.

Is Religion Important?

"A father can give his sons homes and riches, but only the Lord can give them understanding wives" (19:14). Although many students lightly discuss the role of religion in interpersonal relationships, research has shown that religion plays an important role in marriage stability. Some eighteen studies on the correlation between religion and happy and successful marriages have shown that the prospects are better if the couple both belong to a church, if they are married by a clergyman, if they attend Sunday School, and if they attend church two to four times a month. Evidence is in that these religious practices are of great importance.

There are some rather obvious explanations for much of this. Married couples need common and shared interests in certain things they do together. Being a Christian and attending a church and Sunday School helps in these two important areas.

The word religion literally means "to bind," and religion should be a uniting force in marriage. Decide early about your church affiliation. If you belong to different churches you can follow one of the three paths. He can join her church. She can join his church. Or you both join a third church. The important thing is to do something about this before you get married.

Here is a guide to help you evaluate your relationship with a prospective spouse.

THE ADOLESCENT AND HIS FAMILY

"Listen to your father's advice and don't despise an old mother's experience" (23:22).
The parent anxiously watching a stumbling adolescent is mollified when the advice offered from years of adult experience is summarily rejected. If this impasse is to be overcome, we must develop a technique of communication, and one of the most effective might be the process of negotiation.

For a long time the negotiation-communication technique has been used in situations where differences exist—international diplomacy, labor-management disputes, ethnic, or religious controversies. The principle has already been applied to some of the problems of parent-child relationships. The marriage counselor is in many senses an arbitrator; family courts do the same thing; and

ARE YOU READY?

	YES	NO
1. Are you aged at least 20 if a girl or 22 if a boy?	☐	☐
2. Have you known each other for two years?	☐	☐
3. Has your engagement been nine months or more?	☐	☐
4. Do you both belong to the same church?	☐	☐
5. Do you both attend church from two to four times a month?	☐	☐
6. Do your parents approve your prospective mate?	☐	☐
7. Do your friends think this is a wise choice?	☐	☐
8. Are your two backgrounds similar?	☐	☐
9. Have you discussed finances in a future marriage?	☐	☐
10. Do you know how many children you'll plan to have?	☐	☐
11. Have you reached an understanding about your respective roles in marriage?	☐	☐

the psychologist has long found himself as the mediator of the generations. More recently, psychotherapy has developed family therapy which involves mediation.

The following principles may help in the negotiating process:

Maintain your self-control. Much talk by your teenager will sound unreasonable if not downright impertinent, but make some allowances for the brashness of immature youth. If he loses his temper, you descend to his level if you lose yours.

Be prepared to acknowledge your own failures. One father shouted, "I'm right. Even when I'm wrong, I'm right." We adults make plenty of mistakes. If we acknowledge them, our teenager is often ready for dialogue.

One father who had been particularly rough on his son said, "Jim, I was wrong. I shouldn't have lost my temper. I'm sorry." The boy responded, "I shouldn't have taken the car without asking."

When we are willing to acknowledge our failures we discover the truth of the saying, "A man is never stronger than when he's admitting his weaknesses."

COUNSEL TO YOUTH

"I want to warn young men about some problems they will face" (*1:4*).

Proverbs 3:1	*Proverbs 4:21*
Proverbs 3:7	*Proverbs 5:2*
Proverbs 3:11	*Proverbs 6:1*
Proverbs 4:1	*Proverbs 6:6*
Proverbs 4:11	*Proverbs 6:21–22*

Some situations are not negotiable. We can't negotiate whether or not to obey the law. The teenager must do this. This is a painful but necessary boundary that must be set up.

Take time to listen. Remember how much your teenager glorifies communication. He's often convinced he's been on the receiving end for a long time. Now he feels his time has come.

Fight back every impulse to interrupt. Listen, listen, listen. Just give a response of, "Oh," "I see," "You sure have a point there." You may be surprised at the way in which he will talk himself out of some of the ideas that he previously held.

Acknowledge his ability to reason. When he asks "why," it isn't enough simply to say, "Because I say so." Don't downgrade his weak arguments or make sarcastic comments. Use good-natured questions that will help him face his own inconsistencies. Ask him about his recommendations.

Start a new train of thought. "Have you thought of this?" "What will you do if this arises?" Sometimes an anecdote will help, "I once knew a fellow . . ." Reference to a newspaper cartoon or story may help to show that the problem you two are facing is part of the universal human dilemma.

Attack the act, not the person. When junior does something foolish, don't say, "You're so stupid; that's not the way to go about things."

The better way would be, "I love and respect you, but I think that action was wrong, wrong, wrong. Nevertheless I love you, even if I don't like what you're doing?" Learn to negotiate with your adolescents. It will call for patience and understanding, but it will pay off in the long run.

In England's darkest hour, during the early days of

World War 2, British people found themselves embroiled in the Battle of Britain as a numerically superior enemy hurled its combined air strength against their embattled island. England's leader—an old man, the redoubtable Winston Churchill—called on 18-year-old English boys to take their Spitfires and Hurricanes to the skies and fight off the invaders. Speaking about these adolescents, the elderly Churchill said, "Never in the history of human conflict have so many owed so much to so few." Youth and maturity together can similarly ward off the attack on the embattled family of our day and so help to discover its tremendous strengths in building a better society.

PROVERBIAL TEACHINGS ABOUT YOUTH

Proverbs 1:10–12	*Proverbs 17:21*
Proverbs 2:1	*Proverbs 17:25*
Proverbs 3:1–12	*Proverbs 18:22*
Proverbs 4:1–22	*Proverbs 19:14*
Proverbs 4:24–25	*Proverbs 19:26*
Proverbs 6:1–5	*Proverbs 20:20*
Proverbs 6:20–24	*Proverbs 23:19–21*
Proverbs 6:25	*Proverbs 23:22*
Proverbs 7:1–5	*Proverbs 23:24–25*
Proverbs 7:25	*Proverbs 24:21–22*
Proverbs 10:1	*Proverbs 27:11*
Proverbs 13:1	*Proverbs 28:24*
Proverbs 15:20	*Proverbs 30:17*
Proverbs 17:6	*Proverbs 30:18–19*

Proverbs 31:1–7

5

SEX WITHOUT AND WITHIN MARRIAGE

Listen to me, young men, and not only listen but obey; don't let your desires get out of hand; don't let yourself think about her. Don't go near her; stay away from where she walks, lest she tempt you and seduce you.
Proverbs 7:24–25

Probably the most scary public-speaking assignment I ever had was at the Air Force Academy in Colorado Springs, Colorado. I had the privilege of addressing a large gathering of cadets on the subject of "Sex and the Single Man." At the conclusion of my talk, the men formed small groups to discuss the presentation; then each group nominated a spokesman to pose a question to me.

These bright-eyed cadets lined up and one at a time they stepped forward to pose a question. They certainly tested my mental agility, as they probed the ideas of Christian sexual morality I had presented to them. One particularly handsome, clear-eyed young man asked, "How would you like to be a cadet here, not able to marry, living with all these men, and vividly aware of your own demanding sexuality?"

I was immediately ushered into the stark reality of the world of the adolescent conscious of the "hormonal surge" which has pushed his sexuality into a new prominence and confronting him with many questions concerning his own sexual attitudes. The type of question these cadets presented to me might cause some observers to comment on the frankness of "modern youth," but Proverbs is equally frank in its discussion of sexuality. The writing penned as much as 3,000 years ago is as open and frank as any modern publication on human sexuality as it discusses both single sexuality and the place of sex in marriage.

SINGLE SEXUALITY

"Let wisdom hold you back from visiting a prostitute, from listening to her flattery" (7:5).
In focusing attention on sexual temptation, Proverbs presents us with an allegory of two women who vie for a young man's attention. One is the prostitute representing illicit sexual activity. The second is wisdom so often referred to in this book as "she" who comes with common-sense counsel on moral issues. In many ways the same two alternatives face many of us today.

The changes that have taken place in society since the days of Proverbs have compounded the sexual, moral problems faced by young people. New methods of contraception which claim to be almost perfect, new situational ethics stating it is just about impossible to set up standards with circumstances determining what is right and what is wrong, automobiles and apartments providing greater opportunities, a new portrayal through the media of free and easy and apparently glamorous approach to life with the inference that few people maintain high moral standards and "everybody does it." All of these have complicated the decision a young man or young woman must make whether or not to live by the Christian ethic of postponing sexual experiences until after marriage. This old book of Proverbs presents us with some pretty compelling arguments for maintaining what we now see as Christian sexual standards.

1) *Prosmiscuity may leave its mark on personality.*

"But afterwards only a bitter conscience is left to you, sharp as a double-edged sword" (5:4).

The word conscience as used in this passage in *The Living Bible* reminds us of a vital aspect of the human personality. Distinguished psychologist O. Hobart Mowrer has postulated that the most important facet of human personality is a man's value system or conscience. When an individual violates his values, he may manifest a variety of symptoms that will affect both his adjustment to life and his relationships with his fellow men. A long experience in working with this theory has shown that sexual behavior is an area in which adolescents are particularly vulnerable.

One of the most fascinating aspects of the Bible is the manner in which it teaches some of its lessons by presenting a vignette of life that dramatizes a moral principle. Such an incident is seen in the event that sparked Absalom's plan for the assassination of his step-brother, Amnon. Amnon was attracted to his virgin step-sister, Tamar. The infatuation grew in intensity so that Amnon "fell sick" for Tamar and confided to Jonadab, "I love Tamar, my brother Absalom's sister." With connivance of Jonadab, Amnon pretended to be ill and lured Tamar to his home. Despite her desperate pleadings, he sexually assaulted her. After the event came a remarkable sequel: "Then Amnon hated her exceedingly; so that the hatred with which he hated her was greater than the love wherewith he had loved. And Amnon said unto her, Arise, and be gone" (2 Sam. 13:15, KJV).

The change in Amnon's attitude toward Tamar characterizes the sexually-aroused person who, in the heat of emotional desire, will temporarily set aside moral values, but once having violated his value system, his super-ego or conscience begins to punish him. He in turn projects his guilt onto his victim. Here Amnon follows this pattern by throwing Tamar out of his house. The whole episode gives point to the statement of Proverbs, "But afterwards only a bitter conscience is left to you, sharp as a two edged sword" (5:4).

2) *Promiscuity may lead to a pregnancy.*

"Why should you beget children with women of the street?" (5:16).

In Solomon's days, much more than in our own biologically sophisticated era, a pregnancy was an ever-present possibility for promiscuous people. Despite the tremendous advances in the techniques of contraception and the bold assertion that, "No girl has to become pregnant in this enlightened day," a pregnancy is always a live option. Casual contraception is a risky business, and many kids have the strange, distorted view that they do not want to interfere with the naturalness of the experience and take no precautions, making a pregnancy a very real possibility.

If the girl becomes pregnant (and we might note that the girl is the most obvious loser) she is on the horns of a dilemma. Getting married because of a pregnancy is the poorest reason for matrimony. In this so-called enlightened age, she can elect an abortion, a procedure readily available today. However, being intellectually persuaded as to the rationality of the procedure and the adjusting emotionally are two different matters. An abortion may leave a permanent emotional scar.

For many a girl the movement of new life in her body is the fulfillment of a basic maternal urge. If she doesn't desire marriage and can't bring herself to terminate by abortion, she may decide to have the baby. In this instance a portion of her life is lost as she waits out the pregnancy. Then what will she do? Keep the baby and try to rear it, so it lives at a constant disadvantage or adopt it off and become "a mother without joy" as the fruit of her body becomes the beloved property of someone else.

Anyway it goes, the ever-present possibility of pregnancy is in itself a pretty telling argument against promiscuity.

3) *Promiscuity may have physical effects.*

"Lest afterwards you groan in anguish and in shame, when syphilis consumes your body" (5:11).

Sexually promiscuous people are always open to the possibility of infection with a venereal disease. It comes as something of a shock to discover the ancients were aware of the possibilities of such a contingency as is portrayed in this passage. Theoretically, venereal disease is no longer the threat it was formerly because of the effectiveness of new treatments. However, although there has been a temporary medical victory in the sense that there is a weapon that could potentially wipe out venereal disease, war is being lost as medical authorities report rising tides in infection rates. Many authorities believe, the element of fear having been removed, people have become overconfident, and ignorance is now the biggest problem.

It has been said you can catch venereal disease from the waitress, but not in the dining room. For it to be transmitted, two pieces of mucous membrane must be brought into contact. The more promiscuous an individual, the greater the possibility of infection. Venereal disease, with the exception of the common cold, is the most widespread of all disease transmitted from one individual to another, and tragically the rise in incidence has taken place among teenagers. There is no more vivid demonstration of the principle that, "Whatsoever a man sows that shall he also reap," than that found in our own bodies.

4) *Promiscuity may complicate a marriage relationship.*

". . . a woman's husband will be furious in his jealousy" (6:34).

Proverbs contains a series of warnings about the way in which sexual irresponsibility is going to effect marriage. If marriage is precipitated by a pregnancy it may complicate the relationship in later days. Even when a couple is closely attached and the man earnestly vows he will gladly marry in the event of pregnancy, if a forced marriage follows he often has more than a sneaking impression that she could have tricked him into matrimony. One study found that divorce rates were twice as high among couples whose marriage took place after a premarital pregnancy than among those not faced with a premarital pregnancy.

Although at the time of their sexual involvement, many couples are certain they are going to marry, there is "many a slip twixt the cup and the lip." If the relationship collapses and one partner marries, there is the problem of whether to "confess" or not. When confession is made it can sometimes give the partner, when angry, a weapon with which to berate his partner. On the other hand, a marriage with a "skeleton in the closet" has many disadvantages which may burden the relationship. Whatever the case, it would have been better if the relationship had never taken place.

If the premarital sexual experiences were successful, the more routine sex life within marriage may seem somewhat mundane. The premarital experiences took place in stealth and surrounded by excitement; but now come the ordinary day-by-day experiences. Moreover, if the premarital encounter was with some other widely experienced person with a wide repertoire of techniques, the conventional marriage experiences might seem commonplace and unsatisfactory.

One book on "call girls," the most widely experienced of all, tells how some of the girls bathe continuously in an obvious symbolic effort to erase their guilt, even though they consciously deny any such emotions. In marriage counseling it is quite common to find that even when the sexual partners finally marry each other, they frequently bring guilt into the marriage relationship. This will sometimes manifest itself in anxiety, poor sexual adjustment, frigidity, or impotence, which will hinder adjustment in the married sexual experiences.

The crowning blow of all is: that if sex without marriage was all right before the wedding ceremony, it is difficult for a logical person to see why it should not be just as permissible after the event! Thus the groundwork is laid for future infidelity and unfaithfulness.

THE PROVERBIAL PLAN OF SEXUAL CONTROL

In a characteristically practical manner Proverbs not only tells of dangers and the problems but also offers some practical suggestions to help the young person cope with the situation. Four lines of activity are suggested.

1. *Watch your thought life.* "Don't let your desires get out of hand; don't let yourself think about her" (7:25). The principle is laid down in another part of Proverbs, "As he thinketh in his heart so is he" (23:7, KJV). Fundamental to all action is the thought life, for here action is planned. Later the apostle Paul was to present a possible alternative, "Whatsoever things are true, whatsoever things are honest, whatsoever things are just, whatsoever things are pure, whatsoever things are lovely . . . think on these things" (Phil. 4:8, KJV).

Even the wayward thought-life can be brought under control. A man looked at an attractive girl and said to his friend, "I feel attracted to that young lady. Is that sinful?" His friend responded, "While ever it is a fleeting thought I see no problem, but it has possibilities, as Martin Luther said it, 'You cannot help the bird flying over your head, but you can stop them building nests in your hair.' "

Pretty sound advice. Stop the thought from developing, and the battle is more than half won.

2. *Closeness may be dangerous.* "Don't go near her, stay away from where she walks" (7:5). Jesus had an in-

teresting philosophy about situations we get ourselves into. He said on one occasion, "If thy foot or hand offend thee, cut it off and cast it from thee." The use of the word "foot" obviously referred to the places people walked to, went. Did he mean that if a man walked into the wrong place that he should literally cut off his foot? Certainly not. His use of the figure of speech about feet, "cut it off," meant: if you walk into certain places and there you compromise yourself, don't go there; stay away.

So in Proverbs the writer is reminding the young person there are certain places into which he shouldn't go, certain things he shouldn't do, and certain things he may have to forego looking at, because of the possibility of an overwhelming temptation.

3. *Bodily contact builds sexual desire.*

"Spurn the careless kiss" (4:24).

The writer of Proverbs is aware of the potentialities of bodily contact. He would probably be scandalized if he could see the manifold body contact that takes place between young people today as they are pushed toward this type of activity in a sex-saturated culture.

Solomon's warnings are even more applicable today than they were in his day, as young people participate in the activities we refer to as necking, petting, heavy petting, and sundry other expressions. It might be a good idea to use a set of criteria for evaluation these experiences.

Here's a set of criteria for evaluating petting.

(1) Does it mean the same to both of us, or is one person exploiting the other?

(2) Does your partner in this experience see you as a total personality or just a body to be conveniently used?

(3) Do you detach yourselves from the all-important group experiences so significant in developing your personality and continually isolate yourself for your petting activities?

(4) Does this experience leave you wrought up, apprehensive, and wondering about your Christian commitment?

(5) Is it like a habit-forming drug? Do you have to go further and further each time to get the same emotional response?

(6) Could it easily get you into a big mess? "Heavy petting" is foreplay, the prelude to sexual intercourse. Continue the prelude for long enough, and you will reach the point of no return.

Solomon certainly had a point when he warned about the careless kiss. A poet once said:

> *Alas, how things easily go wrong.*
> *A sigh too deep, a kiss too long.*
> *And all is mist and blinding rain*
> *And life is never the same again.*

4. *Take a Counter Action.* "Run from her" (5:7). "Pull back your foot from danger" (4:27). The main way for a young person to handle temptation is to take some action. Do something. Just remaining quiescent and dwelling on the temptation will only allow a person to become further mired in it all. One needs to run, act. Some program of physical exercise could be a tremendous help to any young person who is having a battle with temptation.

Psychologists speak about a psychological mechanism which they call "sublimation," by which some basic drive is turned into another channel. Years ago I conducted church services among the natives on the island of New Guinea and was amazed to hear some of the strange tunes the people had to their hymns. Further inquiries revealed that they had originally been war chants, but missionaries had given the newly converted natives the Christian message of peace for all men, and they sang it to the tune of the primitive war chant. Similarly, the mechanism of sublimation may be used as the powerful sex drive is redirected into new channels. Sigmund Freud, the famous psychologist, was critical of religion but in one letter he wrote to his friend Pfister, with almost a wistful note, he said, "From a therapeutic point of view I can only envy you the possibility of sublimation that religion affords." Religious motivations are vital for sublimation. Psychology can teach us sublimation, but it takes a vital Christian faith to put meaning into it.

SEX IN MARRIAGE

"Let your manhood be a blessing, rejoice in the wife of your youth" (5:18).

Proverbs carries a continuing message concerning the importance of a marriage relationship, and nowhere is this more clearly seen than in the way it highlights a wife's position and responsibility. She is to be a partner to her husband and she is to be the sharer in a good, healthy sex relationship. As with so many other places in the Bible, Proverbs is pro-sex, while at the same time recognizing some of the possible negative aspects of human sexuality.

(1) *Sex is Creative*

There are three things too wonderful for me to understand—no four!

How an eagle glides through the sky.
How a serpent crawls upon a rock.
How a ship finds its way across the heaving ocean.
The growth of love between a man and a girl.

(30:18–19)

The dramatic story of Genesis 1 tells about God's creative activity. As the climax to his work, God created man, "Male and female created he them." This creative activity is followed by the statement that God saw "it was very good." A creative God had brought into existence a creative man to whom he gave the command, "Be fruitful and multiply" (Gen. 1:28, KJV). So humans exercise their sexuality at the command of God. Man and woman can take pride in the fact that God has united them to join with him in creative activity.

As David Mace writes, "In the religion of the Hebrews, as the Old Testament describes it, sex played a central role. It was the means by which a man became a father; and becoming a father was without exception the most important event that happened in his entire life. It was an event, moreover, of profound spiritual significance."

Even many of the biblical restrictions on sexual activity were aimed at a more certain procreation. The book of Leviticus gives a series of injunctions about menstruation. Two significant verses are: "And if a woman have an issue, and her issue in her flesh shall be blood, she shall be put apart seven days: and whosoever toucheth her shall be unclean until the even" (Lev. 15:19, KJV). "But if she be cleansed of her issue then she shall number to herself seven days and after that she shall be clean" (Lev. 15:28, KJV).

One bright sexologist got to work with his calculations and concluded that husbands and wives following this regimen would recommence sexual relations fourteen days from the onset of menstruation. In all probability both partners, after such a period of abstinence, would be highly motivated.

In the menstrual cycle this is the most probable period of ovulation; consequently the time when the wife would most likely become pregnant. Small wonder in 1 Chronicles 27:23 there is the statement, "The Lord said he would increase Israel like to the stars of the heavens."

If these writers could have looked on to the future insights of science, they would have discovered that the basic chemical action of sex-related hormones is such that it pushes man toward creativity, even if this does not take the form of procreation. Observers of animal life have long discovered that in terms of energy, sex hormones must be the most powerful substance known to man. When two rats are compared, one castrated and the other normal, the normal is more vigorous, ambitious, and aggressive. If they are placed in separate cages on exercise wheels, the normal rat will run up to seventy times the distance of the castrated rat.

It is fairly easy to conclude just how important this hormonal energy is in the creative life of man.

The creative aspect of human sexuality is the first and foremost note of the Bible showing that it is pro-sex rather than anti-sex, as has often been maintained.

(2) *Sex Is for Union*

Her husband can trust her and she will richly satisfy his needs. (31:11)

The Genesis story of creation tells of a series of God's creative acts, and after each of these comes the statement, "And God saw that it was good"; then suddenly there comes the statement, "It was not good." "It was not good that man should be alone." So God created a helpmeet for man and gave the command, "They twain shall become one flesh."

My sex drive helps me realize I am incomplete. I need my wife. And in this relationship we bring to each other some of the most pleasurable experiences known to mankind. After all the discussion about the problems of sexual temptation, the writer of Proverbs comes up with an interesting suggestion.

> *Let a young wife be your joy,*
> *a lovely hind, a charming doe is she;*
> *let her breasts give you rapture*
> *   let her love ever ravish you*
> *Why be ravished with a loose creature,*
> *   and embrace the bosom of another woman?*
> *(5:18–20, Moffatt)*

Here is counteraction, fighting fire with fire—certainly an unexpected course of action advocated by a book that is supposed to say sex is dirty.

A similar idea of the function of sex is found in the Song of Solomon, traditionally seen as the product of Solomon's hand. In the *Moffatt* translation the bridegroom says:

> *You stand there straight as a palm,*
> *with breasts like clusters of fruit;*
> *methinks I will climb that palm,*
> *taking hold of the boughs!*
> *Oh may your breasts be clusters of fruit,*
> *and your breath sweet as an apple!*
> *(Song of Sol. 7:7–8, Moffatt)*

And the bride responds:

> *I am my darling's and he—*
> *he is longing for me.*
> *Come away to the fields, O my darling,*
> *let us sleep in the blossoms of henna,*
> *and hie us at dawn to the vineyards,*
> *to see if the vines are a-budding*
> *if their blossoms are open,*
> *if pomegranates bloom;*
> *and there I will give you caresses of love.*
> *(Song of Sol. 7:10–12, Moffatt)*

The Bible goes on to remind husbands and wives that they have a sexual obligation to each other, speaking of which later Paul says, "Defraud ye not, one another."

(3) *Sex Is Not to Be Exploited*

"A man who commits adultery is an utter fool, for he destroys his own soul" (6:32).

Because sex is such a powerful force in human personality, it can be exploited. The Bible anticipates this trend.

The Decalogue or Ten Commandments has been a model for lawmakers across the centuries. It is sometimes divided into two segments. Six of the commandments have to do with a man's relationship to his fellowman. Of the six that refer to man, three—or half of them—relate to the sexual content of life.

The Fifth Commandment is, "Honor thy father and they mother." The child is to see in his parents the model of filial relationships. They committed themselves to each other, and as a result of the commitment the child was born.

This setting sounds strangely modern. In more recent days Masters and Johnson have done some rather esoteric investigations into sex. When quizzed about the best way to come at sex eduation, Dr. Masters replied that the best home-style sex education is exposure to spontaneous warmth and affection between parents. "There is nothing that teaches about sex half so much as Pop patting Mom's fanny as he walks by her in the kitchen. Obviously she loves it, and the kids watch and say, 'Boy, that's for me.' That's sex education as it can be done in the home. I don't mean that Mom and Pop shouldn't answer questions about the birds and the bees. They should."

The Seventh Commandment, "Thou shalt not commit adultery" (Ex. 20; Deut. 5:18), is the basis of a good monogamous relationship within which the husband and wife are to maintain a fundamental loyalty to each other and thus provide a stable framework within which children will have security as they grow and develop.

The Tenth Commandment in some ways looks on to the ministry of Jesus who emphasized the thought-life. It aims not just at regulating his outward actions but also his inner motivations. It says, "Thou shalt not covet thy neighbor's house, thou shalt not covet thy neighbor's wife, nor his manservant, nor his maidservant, nor his ox, nor his ass, nor anything that is thy neighbor's" (Ex. 20:17, KJV). Notice the way the list includes the things common to everyday family life: house, servants, animals. A man is not only forbidden to steal but even to consider the possibility. At the head of all this stands a man's wife. She is his most precious possession; to take her from him would be to bring down the family.

When Mrs. Farmer returned rather unexpectedly to her home and stumbled upon her daughter, Marie, in a compromising situation with her boyfriend, James, she felt the time had come for a mother-daughter talk.

Mrs. Farmer tried to remain objective, struggling to retain control over her emotions. Although she was a church member and a devout Christian, she deliberately refrained from mentioning religion or the Bible in her discussion. Then Marie raised the issue, "I've just been waiting for you to quote the Bible to me, Mother."

"You have?"

"Yes, James and I have had some long talks about these things, and we've both agreed love is the important thing, and the Bible doesn't really have anything to say on the matter."

Somewhat taken aback Mrs. Farmer responded, "What about the Seventh Commandment, 'Thou shalt not commit adultery'?"

"Oh, Mother, there you are, all mixed up like I thought. Adultery is when one of the partners is married. It doesn't refer to unmarried people."

Of course, Marie was mistaken. There are over twenty references which warn against fornication, such as, "Flee fornication" (1 Cor. 6:18, KJV). The New Testament abounds in warnings against unrestrained, exploitive sex.

Scripture statements may all too easily be misapplied. In any discussion on masturbation, someone is sure to call attention to the verse, "I say unto you, That whosoever looketh on a woman to lust after her hath committed adultery with her already in his heart" (Matt. 5:28, KJV). But a better approach to this verse is to see that

Jesus is warning against looking upon a person just as a body to be conveniently used. We must see another person not as a sex object but a total personality.

Sex is good, the Bible says so. A recent book by Harry Hollis, Jr., is titled *Thank God for Sex,* and all the evidence goes to show this is the attitude Christians should have towards this God-given factor in human personality.

In Taoism there is a stress upon two forces—yin and yang. In Taoism everything in the universe shows the interplay of these forces and contains their characteristics in varying degrees. The yang is the positive or masculine force. Everything in the universe contains both forces. At one time the yin may be stronger and another time the yang. In marriage the masculine and the feminine forces constantly interrelate as a meaningful part of the whole.

Sex is meant to be a cohesive factor in marriage. Proverbs reminds us that all too frequently it can be misused. Three times in the Old Testament is found the exhortation, "Thou shall not see the kid in his mother's milk." While there is something repulsive about cooking an animal in the milk of its mother, it seems as if there is a principle here. The principle—you won't use that which was meant to minister life for the purpose of administering death. Sex is like this, meant to be a creative power; it can all too easily be turned in the wrong direction.

Sir Walter Scott's *Kenilworth* tells the story of the Countess of Leicester. Her husband, a nobleman in the court of Queen Elizabeth, didn't want England's virgin queen to know about his secret marriage, so he kept his wife a prisoner in his country castle. Outside her room was a trap door supported by bolts. If the bolts were removed the trap door was held in place by springs but would immediately collapse under the tiniest weight.

The two guards, Foster and Varney, had removed the bolts, and later Foster heard the sound of horses' hooves on the pavement and the sound of whistling, as when the Earl returned to the castle.

In an instant the Countess's door was flung open. She rushed onto the trap and fell to her death.

Varney's voice came through the window, "Is the bird caught? Is the deed done?"

Foster suddenly realized it was not the Earl at all. Varney had ridden in whistling like the Earl. The Countess rushing out to meet her beloved had perished.

Foster turned on Varney and said, "Oh, if there is a judgment in heaven, thou hast deserved it, and will meet it! Thou hast destroyed her by her best affections. It is a seething of a kid in his mother's milk."

Sex should be sacred. To pervert its use is the seething of the kid in its mother's milk.

PROVERBS ON SEX

Proverbs 4:23–27   *Proverbs 7:21–23*
Proverbs 5:1–6   *Proverbs 7:24–27*
Proverbs 5:7–14   *Proverbs 9:13–18*
Proverbs 5:15–21   *Proverbs 11:22*
Proverbs 6:25–31   *Proverbs 22:14*
Proverbs 6:32–35   *Proverbs 23:26–28*
Proverbs 7:5–12   *Proverbs 30:20*
Proverbs 7:13–20   *Proverbs 30:18–19*
Proverbs 31:11

6

THE WISDOM OF THE YEARS

Wisdom gives a long, good life.   *Proverbs 3:16*

The message of Proverbs tells of the glories of old age. The proverbial philosophy about aging might not really sit well today in the United States where we are obsessed with the worship of youth.

In part, perhaps because we are a young country just entering into our third century, we have a vague idea everything new and young must be good, and everything old must be obsolete and jettisoned. How widely this contrasts with the East where age is venerated and life's experiences prized. In a country like England, the old, the traditional is valued. Maurois, speaking of the election of elderly Disraeli as prime minister in his later years, says, "No people are more sensitive than the English to the beauty wherewith time can adorn an object; they love an old statesman, born and polished by the struggle, as they love old leather and old wood." This is not so in the *new* world. Bulldoze away the monuments of the past and build our energy-devouring steel and glass monuments in the name of progress, and like so many horses being turned out to grass let's get rid of our valuable, seasoned, experienced members of society. Proverbs comes with the message of the glory of age.

Proverbs itself is a compilation of the wisdom of the

past carefully gathered together and compiled so that it can be passed on to succeeding generations. And this is as it should be. The older segment of society is responsible for passing on the legacy of the race, so in Proverbs is the statement, "An old man's grandchildren are his glory" (17:6). Most of us are intuitively aware of this responsibility, but the vital necessity of considering one's family and making provision for future generations was brought home to me personally by a preacher of sorts.

I am something of a connoisseur of preachers. I've been listening to them for many years. Let me hear one of those pulpiteers for a few minutes, and I will tell you whether he is preaching someone else's sermon, has been dipping into a book of ready-made outlines, is stringing a series of inappropriate stories together, or whether he is really a master of hermeneutics and homiletics and has the delivery techniques of the pulpit orator.

Despite this wide experience I have to hand it to a humble seller of insurance who was positively the best preacher I've ever heard. It happened on a church picnic, of all places. Down by the beach we had worked our way through a massive table of food and that strange afterglow that comes with the sinking sun had spread its spell over us. The enthusiastic insurance man saw his opportunity and proceeded to tell us about selling a man an insurance policy. Having convinced his prospect, the salesman agreed—rather foolishly, it turned out—to go with his new client to break the news to his wife.

To the insurance man's dismay he discovered the wife was not impressed with what she considered the remote possibility of $50,000 while she paid the premiums from her budget. Moreover, for some years now she had longed for a mink coat which was much more tangible than a possible insurance settlement. So the deal fell through, and our loquacious friend lost the sale.

Of course, the inevitable happened, and the man

collapsed on the street one noon and died from a heart attack. The insurance agent called at the home to offer his condolences, and as he was leaving the widow thanked him for coming by.

It was the salesman's moment. He paused, I saw his eyes moisten; then with a choke in his voice he reported the lady's very words.

"That fur coat was the most expensive present I ever received; it cost me $50,000."

As I sat at the picnic table in the hush of his statement, my first impulse was to make a humorous remark and break the spell, but on second thought I realized this man, with his simple story and probably ulterior motive, had abruptly ushered us into the reality of the one certain experience we all face—death. For those who are advanced in years the possibility of death becomes increasingly real, and people who have judiciously prepared for the future and saved their money will pass on their hard-earned dollars to their children, proud that they have had some part in helping them get established in life.

While most people are aware of responsibility to their children, when we move to the proverb that tells us, "A child's glory is its father," the rising generation is not so sure for it is very much concerned about its peers rather than the older generation.

The worship of youth may have reached its climax in an event at the 1976 Olympic Games. Olga Korbut had been the gymnastic star at the 1972 Munich Games when she had won two gold medals and a silver. Following this triumph the crowds had flocked to see her perform. Now, at the "advanced" age of 21 in Montreal, Canada, for the 1976 games, Olga sat on the side of the arena as 4'11" Nadia Comaneci, aged 14, turned in perfect 10.00 gymnastic performances on seven occasions.

As the event proceeded Olga refused to watch her

younger rival in action, burst into tears, and during one of Comaneci's perfect efforts slowly, but pointedly, walked halfway across the auditorium to the water fountain. One observer stated that her face was at that moment, "haggard beyond middle age." At 21 she was out of it. Away with the elderly 21-year-older—bring on the 14-year-older!

One of the classical arguments for the immortality of man is referred to as the teleological argument. It claims man is continually developing and though his body begins to wear out with advancing years, his moral progress continues. Consequently the argument goes, there must be life after death. It sounds something like the statement in Proverbs, "The glory of young men is their strength: of old men, their experience" (20:29). By failing to recognize the great value of this moral growth and experience we are denying humans their rightful recognition.

When the youthful Michelangelo was summoned to the Medici palace, he hoped it was for a commission to carve a statue from the durable marble with which he loved to work. Imagine his disappointment when he was asked to carve an enormous snowman. It was the whim of Giulumio, then the tyrant of Florence, who on the morning of his birthday had requested, "the greatest snowman ever made." So he who loved the solid, durable marble labored on a sculpture that melted away even as he worked. In many ways a society that fails to recognize the value of citizens at the height of their moral and intellectual growth and experience is guilty of the same crime.

Worse still it seems that a certain segment of youthful society has seen the older generation as easy victims for their aggressive impulses. Living in their own houses or apartments seems to be the ideal arrangement for many oldsters who have carefully saved their money and reside in a house that is the repository of the memories of the years. Rather unfortunately this has made them vulnerable subjects for what has come to be known in the language of crime as a "crib job." The term is used by young punks who say robbing the elderly is like taking candy from a baby.

Reports from across the nation tell the sordid story. In New York two 16-year-old step brothers tried to rape a 75-year-old woman after robbing her. In Seattle police report an 18 percent increase in crime against the elderly this year alone. In Detroit an 80-year-old woman was attacked in a supermarket parking lot by three youths. From San Francisco a social worker commented on the attacks of the elderly, "They're weak and vulnerable. They always have some money with them and are usually too shaken by the attack to remember clearly." [1]

Tragically, the assailants have learned they can get away with these brutal attacks. New York police estimate for every crime reported against the elderly there are some thirty victims who don't say anything. When the crime is reported and an arrest is made, a strange bias in favor of the young becomes evident. Prosecutors in New York are not allowed to reveal a suspect's juvenile arrest record. One man charged with beating and robbing an 82-year-old woman was released, the law preventing the judge from being told that the suspect had a record of sixty-seven previous arrests, including one charge of murdering a 92-year-old man!

The result of all this is that many elderly people have developed a fortress mentality and spend their time holed up in their homes, ready to repel an attacker. Hans Kable, 78, and his wife, Emma, 76, were attacked by young thugs who repeatedly stabbed Emma in the face with a fork and demanded money she didn't have. The Kables laid out their best clothes on a bed, then committed suicide, leaving a pathetic note, "We don't want to live with fear anymore."

But what of the place of the elderly in our work force? The immediate answer in many minds is to suggest the "humane" possibility that once people have reached a certain age, say 60 or 65, the best thing to do is to retire them and let them enjoy the fruits of their labors. This is all well and good for *some* people, and there certainly should be the possibility of voluntary retirement. Yet, the moment we make it mandatory we fly in the face of all we have learned about individual differences and the necessity of seeing each individual as unique. Along with the discriminations we have talked about for so long, race discrimination and sex discrimination, we have perpetrated age discrimination.

The inequity of our attitude towards the elderly who do not wish to retire is clearly a nullification of the virtue of honest work. The more diligent a person, the more likely it is that he will have difficulty in adjusting to the period of life we call retirement. If a man has been careless about his responsibilities, looked for the easy way out, been absent from work at every opportunity, then he will move easily into a retirement which will become a virtual paradise for him. He can sit back and let others periodically accept responsibility, complaining that he's not receiving his fair share of this world's goods. On the other hand, if he has been conscientious and diligent, proud of his work, the idea of being turned out to pasture will be difficult for him to take. Obviously, our attitude towards the elderly is teaching our young people the wrong lesson. Ideally, we should be creating in them the idea that they should apply themselves to their work, and that hard work will bring its reward. The current lesson is that hard work will bring an extra penalty to life. If you work hard and are conscientious, then retirement will be most difficult indeed. Fortunately the Congress has passed new legislation allowing a worker to retire at 70, if he desires.

Add to all this the importance of the action principle, and the problem is compounded. Action is an indication of life, as Dr. Leithauser says, "Absolute inactivity is death." To prolong life we need action; to shorten it, idleness. Fitness specialist Kenneth Cooper says of the human heart, "Ironically the heart works faster and less efficiently when you give it little to do than it does when you make demands upon it. It is a remarkable machine."

One interesting theory about the human heart is that each individual is born with a certain number of heartbeats—when these are used up that's it. From this contention, it would be easy to get the idea that having a limited number of heartbeats, it would be best to take it easy and save them up. Not so says Dr. Kurland, "Even if you hold to this belief, the way to slow your heart rate and stave off that last dub-dub is not by taking it easy, but by exercising. While your heart does speed up during stress—often more than three times its normal pace—the accumulative effect of exercise reduces the resting heart rate by as much as 50 percent. The heart of an athlete in prime condition may pump fewer than forty beats per minute at rest." [2]

If we follow this theory through it offers some interesting possibilities. Supposing an individual's heart beats at 72 beats per minute for 70 years it will mean he will have 2,650,838,400 beats in a lifetime. If he gets out of condition and his heart rate moves up to 90 beats a minute, a 70-year-old life span would demand 3,313,548,000 heart beats. On the other hand a person in good condition will have a heart rate of 60 beats per minute, and his heart will beat 2,419,032,000 in a 70-year life period. Based on this theory, the individual in condition will have 7.34 more years of life than the average person and 28.35 years more than the person in bad condition. There's no excuse for avoiding activity. It doesn't wear us out but rather gives us an extension of life.

As threatening as the onset of old age is to a man, it pales into insignificance when compared with that faced by a woman contemplating the possible loss of physical attractiveness. Proverbs portrays the woman who realizes, "Charm can be deceptive and beauty doesn't last" (31:30), but has found the solution to her problem, "She is a woman of strength and dignity and has no fear of old age" (31:25). The reading Proverbs 31 shows her to be a woman of enormous capacity as she works as a supervisor (31:15), realtor (31:16), seamstress (31:9), buyer and seller (31:14), weaver (31:13), horticulturist (31:16). Small wonder the writer climaxes the passage with the statement, "Praise her for the many things she does" (31:31). All of this activity may give us a clue to her lack of fear of old age.

One experience dramatized forever for me the problem of capital punishment. I was conducting a conference for chaplains at a penitentiary in which an execution was about to take place. The chaplain of the institution was in and out of the conference as he periodically tried to calm the distraught mother of the man about to be executed. As preparations moved toward the awful moment, a tension permeated the whole prison population, and the chaplain assumed a new importance in this crisis hour. If the prisoner struggled and had to be wrestled into the electric chair it would throw the whole institution into an emotional turmoil. It became a major responsibility of the chaplain to convince the condemned man that he should go quietly.

Questions raced through my mind. Go quietly. But it's his life, his only life. Does anyone have the right to tell him to surrender his one and only life so that other people will feel better?

Having watched a number of people being retired or turned out to pasture, I frequently see the same elaborate charade with the message, "Go quietly, please. You may be giving up your life but please don't distress us. Don't raise any questions, slip away, don't make us feel bad."

The throw-away attitude toward our older citizens

means we are losing one of our most valuable assets—human experience. "A hoary head is a crown of glory" (16:31, KJV).

One of the most poignant verses in the Scriptures is found in Psalms where it says, "Cast me not off in the time of old age, forsake me not when my strength faileth" (Psalm 71:9, KJV) and it immediately raises the issue of just what we should do with our elderly citizens, particularly when they find life difficult to handle.

The institution we call the nursing home in our nation should be ideal with oldsters enjoying the companionship of people their own age and with adequate medical care readily available. A survey by a committee of the U.S. Senate reveals the situation is not always so good. Medical care in nursing homes was shown to be both "miserably inadequate" and "ridiculously expensive." Many of the "inmates" of these homes were virtually prisoners with no one interested in visiting them. After its wide investigation the committee concluded that if the federal government subsidized married couples to care for their parents in their homes it would be improved care, and "taxpayers would save greatly since it costs more to care for parents in nursing homes than in their own children's homes." It has taken our legislators a long time to come around full cycle and return to a biblical idea.

How different is the situation in Proverbs where the children have a clear and unmistakable obligation to care for their parents, as is still the custom in some other parts of the world. While conducting a conference in Hong Kong, I was interviewed on radio, and my questioner asked my opinion about the Chinese family. I told him we were greatly impressed when we arrived at the airport and found a large group of people assembled to welcome us. Our family had befriended a Chinese student in the U.S., and his whole family had turned out to welcome us—mother and father, aunts and uncles, grandmother, and sundry other relations. It seemed to me that here was a beautiful example of the solidarity of the extended family. The interviewer promptly replied, "That's because we don't have social security. A man must have a large, cohesive family to care for him when he is old." It might be a good idea and certainly seems to be the concept in Proverbs which contains a warning such as, "A son who mistreats his father and mother is a public disgrace" (19:26). And when we look at the nursing home situation it seems clear that children could probably provide the very best kind of care possible for the elderly.

One respected jurist, discussing the problems of awarding custody of the children to parents, said, "I've remembered hundreds of cases in which parents had gone to unusual extremes to gain custody of the children." Then, in a solemn twist, he went on to add rather sadly, "I've never found a single case in which there was a contest by children for the custody of their parents." And by our attitudes toward many of the elderly we have lost some of our best assets, as is seen in the following case of Dr. Duggar.

At seventy years of age, Dr. Duggar was compelled to retire from the University of Wisconsin. He left under protest, pointing out he bowled every week, took long walks, and played golf, but all his protests fell on unresponsive ears. It was the policy of the institution that retirement at seventy was mandatory. His life of research was at an end.

Some of Dr. Duggar's former students had a higher opinion of the older professor's abilities and suggested to their employers, Lederle Laboratories, that the former professor should be engaged as a consultant employed in independent research. As the professor worked in research with molds, he developed a remarkable antibiotic, Aureomycin, which effectively controls more than fifty serious maladies. He continued on to develop Tetracycline, the most widely prescribed of all antibiotics which controls, among other things, streptococcus, pneumonia, staphylococcus, typhus, and syphilis.

Because of an arbitary policy, the University had denied itself the services of a brilliant researcher and stands as a warning against such rigid ideas. For long enough we have been talking about the importance of considering individual differences in children. Surely the time has come for us to spend some time contemplating the individual differences in adults. Particularly oldsters.

PROVERBIAL OLD AGE

Proverbs 3:1–2   *Proverbs 19:26*
Proverbs 3:16   *Proverbs 20:29*
Proverbs 16:31   *Proverbs 31:25*
Proverbs 17:6   *Proverbs 31:30*

7

THE TEMPTATION OF TEMPER

*As the churning of cream yields butter, and a
blow to the nose causes bleeding, so anger causes quarrels.*
Proverbs 30:33

News has come of a town in Missouri where they celebrate "Lizzie Borden Day" in the hope of rehabilitating the memory of that woman. The citizens claim Lizzie has been maligned. Despite all these efforts, Lizzie Borden has been immortalized in the little piece of doggerel:

> *Lizzie Borden took an ax,*
> *And gave her father forty whacks,*
> *When the job was neatly done*
> *She gave her mother forty-one.*

While the idea of Lizzie's traditionally described behavior is repulsive to most of us, we must face the fact of conflict within the family which has become so bad that it was referred to in an article as "the family, the cradle of violence." Some studies have shown that family members abuse each other physically more often than do unrelated individuals. Just a few years ago the *New York Times* carried two articles, one on family violence and the other on the conflict in Northern Ireland. Comparison between the two articles showed that in one six month's period in New York about as many people were murdered by their relatives as had been killed in the three-and-a-half years of conflict in Northern Ireland.

Another study showed that family fights are the largest single category of police calls and that "violence in the home" deserves at least as much attention as "crime in the streets." Moreover police hate and fear family conflict for two reasons. There's little glamor to such a call and family conflicts are particularly dangerous as an emotion-charged family member turns on the representative of the law who dares to intervene in what is generally considered a purely private matter.

All of these considerations of what might be called "crimes of passion" give point to the large portion of the book of Proverbs which is given over to the discussion of such subjects as temper and anger. The box in this chapter indicates there are some twenty or more direct references to these subjects and many more indirect statements.

THAT EMOTIONAL EARLY-WARNING SYSTEM

"There is more hope for a fool than for a man of quick temper" (29:20).
Proverbs has its constant focus on wisdom, and the foolish person is the low man on the totem pole, but Solomon sees yet a lower status for the man of temper. One of the reasons for this may be that the hot-tempered individual never can consider them.

Harry Fontaine is hanging a picture for his wife. An industrious businessman, he is the despair of his mate when it comes to household chores. In fact, he rather prides himself on his lack of domestic skills and often brags that he doesn't know which end of the hammer to hold. But today it is different.

By leaving the picture in an obvious place where he had nearly fallen over it, his helpmate had been able to offer a subtle suggestion and then appear pleasantly surprised when he walked in carrying his seldom-used tools and announced his intention to "get this picture on the wall."

The little woman works hard at keeping him motivated.

"Honey, that's wonderful. Not only the best businessman in the city but a handyman as well," she murmurs.

"Oh, shucks, it's nothing." But Harry has a pretty good feeling. "How's that? Seems like a pretty good spot to me." He holds the picture in a trial position and awaits the final word of approval.

"Just a bit too high, honey. Mother always said you had high ideas . . ."

Harry's interest in picture hanging evaporates. He labors through the rest of the chore in the most half-hearted manner. "Mother always said . . ." does something to Harry.

Like so many of us, Harry has an "Emotional Early-Warning System." As soon as some words cross the threshold of our hearing, the red lights flash, and the alarm bells begin to clang.

The exact moment some Republicans hear "Democrat" or an industrialist hears "union" or there comes to our ears a name or concept about which we fell strongly, the Emotional Early-Warning System goes into action.

Even such a highly developed and intricate radar system as that spreading across North America can misinterpret a harmless object as being a threatening invader. A man's Emotional Early-Warning System may be triggered by one word and prevent him from hearing the rest of the statement.

The wife's word "mother" may fire an explosion and keep hubby from hearing that his mother-in-law has drawn her will in his favor. A message that the representative from the Internal Revenue Department would like an interview can lead to a noncooperative response which will keep the professional man from learning there is a better way to figure his income tax.

One researcher in the industrial field gives an example of the Emotional Early-Warning System in industry. The foreman greets one of his men: "How's the job coming, George?"

Interpretation 1—Simon Legree is checking up on me again.

Interpretation 2—"He's really interested in how I'm doing."

Interpretation 3—"Oh, oh, has he found out that I punched Bill Mott's time card this morning?"

Number 2 might have been the true interpretation, but George will never know, and it doesn't matter what his foreman says, for it will always be misinterpreted.

The mature family member faces the reality of the Emotional Early-Warning System and works at developing techniques for handling this troublesome distortion point in family communication. Here are some pointers:

Distrust your initial reactions. Some people boast about the accuracy of first impressions, but most of these are notoriously inaccurate.

Fight for time before you respond. Don't make impulsive responses.

Forget about the appearance of irritating manner, accent, bombastic or self-effacing attitude. Don't think so much of who is speaking but what he is saying.

If certain words or ideas upset you, write them down and examine them carefully. Ask yourself why. Discuss them with a friend.

Be willing to evaluate a new or unusual idea. Try to see both sides.

As much as you may dislike the idea that you hear, look for some positive aspects of it.

Duly considering all the dangers that a short fuse brings with it, another proverb has special relevance: "It is better to be slow-tempered than famous; it is better to have self-control than to control an army" (16:32).

CONTROL BY TANTRUM

"The fool who provokes his family to anger and resentment will finally have nothing worthwhile left. He shall be the servant of a wiser man" (11:29).

Few of us can witness a violent expression of emotions and not be awed by it. Children learn this early in life and proceed to take advantage of the technique of intimidating by crying, screaming, holding their breath, kicking, and punching. Many parents feel completely helpless in the face of these emotional outbursts and capitulate to the child's demands, thus rewarding him and reinforcing his behavior. Children learn quickly and rapidly master the skill of managing by tantrum. The lesson so learned may be carried over into later life.

The child-learner may now become the child-teacher and turn on his or her parents, teaching them the skills of managing by tantrum. Mrs. Burns, mother of three, aged 8, 7, and 5 respectively, sometimes gets the impression that her family is in a perpetual state of riot. She keeps urging the children, "Hold it down," but they pay little or no attention to her pleas. When she can stand it no longer, she steadily begins to raise her voice until she finds herself yelling.

Mrs. Burns confides in her friend, Mrs. Zimmerman, "After it's all over I feel bad about it, all stirred up, head aching, and I wonder how much the people in the other apartments heard. But it seems to be the only way I can control them."

The children have taught Mrs. Burns to communicate strong emotional expressions as a means of managing her offspring and sometimes seem to take particular pleasure in provoking mother to these expressions. Proverbs says it, "A man without self control is as defenseless as a city with broken down walls" (25:28).

Most people in the common experiences of relationship at their places of employment or social events keep their emotions under control, but when they get home the restraints are off, and the situation may be quite different.

Robert Green's work, for example, is demanding, and he tries to be fair in his dealings with the other employees, but his frustrations mount. When he gets home, he has a very low irritation level.

The Green household has learned about daddy's hair-trigger reaction, so Mrs. Green prepares the family for father's return, making sure the paper is in place near his favorite chair and that all the children are warned of his approach. Green is surprised when his brother, Harold, comes to stay with them a few days and comments on Green's entrance into the house: "I've gotta give it to you, Robert, you've really trained your family. As Patty [Mrs. Green] gets them ready for your entrance, 'Be sure your father's chair is in the right place,' 'Where's the paper?' 'Don't make any noise when daddy arrives,' I have a feeling some Oriental potentate is being give a royal welcome."

The remark leaves Robert with a strange feeling about the way in which he arrives home. He begins to question his attitude and the image he is communicating to the members of his family.

Read Proverbs 11:29 again!

WHO NEEDS IT?

"There is more hope for a fool than for a man of quick temper" (29:20).

For those who require it, a beautiful rationalization is at

hand, and it has an apparently sound psychological theory behind it.

Harrison Taylor is annoyed with Genevieve, his wife, who has finally admitted overspending the budget so she could get the cute little dresses on sale at Neiman-Marcus.

"But honey, can't you see I saved fifty dollars by buying while they were on sale?"

"Saved fifty dollars! What nonsense! I am sick to death of spending money to save money."

"Do you want your wife to go around wearing old clothes?"

"My dear, you've got more clothes than any other three women. There are dresses in your closet that you've never worn twice."

"I'm surprised at you, Harrison, but I should have known. You have always been a tightwad."

"What do you mean, a tightwad?"

So the exchange gets more heated at Harrison and Genevieve's house as they enter into a verbal slugfest.

The following evening they have a long talk, and Genevieve snuggles up to Harrison, "I'm so glad I took those psychology courses. Isn't it good the way we can really express ourselves and drain off our emotions? Our quarrel has been a therapeutic experience."

Taylor—still hurting at the memory of Genevieve's facile and tart tongue that was able to deliver stinging blows —wonders.

The validity of Genevieve's idea that expression of emotions helps to drain them has both proponents and opponents. There are some good reasons to doubt this premise. From observations it seems that constant expression of emotions not only doesn't drain the emotions but may reinforce these reactions. If action brings on feeling, this may simply bring on a more intensive feeling.

Albert Bandura's study of aggression has raised many questions about the validity of the catharsis hypothesis. Children who were permitted to practice aggressive behavior in the hope that the activity might be reduced have maintained the behavior at the same level or actually increased its frequency. Similarly, with adults given opportunities to shock other people under non-retaliative conditions, the more aggressive the behaviors the more punitive they became. Other studies indicate people who ventilate their hostility became increasingly hostile.

SOME RESULTS

"A wise man controls his temper. He knows that anger causes mistakes" (14:29).

Angry outbursts can have a number of bad effects. As we have noted, the subject learns and practices the wrong skill; he learns how he can intimidate people by these emotional blasts. In the second place he successfully alienates the objects of his wrath from him so that he comes to live an increasingly isolated existence as people learn to avoid him. The subject is also affected internally. John Hunter, the former anatomist, used to say, "My life is in the hands of any villain who cares to annoy me," and violent expression of anger can take its toll on the human frame.

Then there are the lessons the angry person is teaching, particularly the angry parent. Proverbs has an admonition, "Don't envy violent men. Don't copy their ways (3:31). We have long known that children learn from the models they observe. One study showed many parents of battered children had themselves been battered children. They had learned the lessons that come from observing a model. Every time you have a fit of temper or anger you are teaching your children how to be angry.

Above everything else, what does it do to the family unit? Take the case of Charla and Jack Donovan. Jack has a hair-trigger reaction, and this in turn sparks something in Charla. In telling her story Charla says, "He gets mad and flies off at me. I stand it for a while; then I become vividly aware of the injustice of his attitude, and I strike back at him. The situation deteriorates, and sometimes we stay mad at each other for several days, and it all started over a triviality. Our whole family stays stirred up for days." A family is an interacting unit and, in the process of expressing these negative emotions, we hurt the ones we love best of all.

One of the self-help groups which has been so effective in working with ex-psychiatric hospital patients and people with emotional problems calls itself Recovery, Inc. The brainchild of Dr. Low, a psychiatrist, it is completely non-professional, using laymen and women and utilizing easily grasped terms to help the members of their group understand the problems with which they are grappling. The concept of temper looms large in their discussions.

In the theory of Recovery, temper is the greatest single problem in life. Dr. Low says that temper is of two types. When an individual feels someone has done him wrong, he is gripped by angry or vicious temper. It appears as resentment, impatience, indignation, disgust, hatred. If the person feels he is wrong and has failed, he experiences fearful or retreating temper. The way out of these temper spells is to take three steps. First of all comes the realization of the moment of temper. This is sabotage. The individual then spots his temper. Having spotted it, he moves on and gets into the process of what is known as "moving one's muscles."

Recovery, Inc., may be recovering an insight which is widely discussed in the Bible and is frequently mentioned in the book of Proverbs, which reminds us, "A wise man controls his temper. He knows that anger causes mistakes" (14:29).

AN EIGHT-FOLD PROGRAM

"A man without self-control is as defenseless as a city with broken down walls" (25:28).

(1) Recognize you are angry or emotionally upset. It is part of the business of living. "Be angry and sin not."

(2) Pinpoint the reason for your anger. Realize who you are mad at. Don't project anger about the office to your wife and children who had nothing to do with these situations. If you are often mad at yourself, face your own foolish mistakes.

(3) Don't be a martyr. You must accept some responsibility for what has happened. William Blake, speaking about anger, said:

> I was angry with my friend,
> I told my wrath, my wrath did end.
> I was angry with my foe
> I told him not, my wrath did grow.

What did this anonymous person tell his friend? If he pointed out his own irresponsibility and said in all honesty, "I have looked over my behavior, and I can see I made some wrong moves," he probably would soon feel better.

Accept your own humanness. Realize when you have failed, and you will feel a lot better about the situation.

(4) Try physical activity. An emotional arousal is a preparation for physical activity. This mechanism prepared primitive man to fight or flee; you may be able to do neither. Work off the adrenaline that has readied your body. Try a walk, jog, work out in the gym. One salesman reported a visit to the driving range where he saw obstreperous clients' faces on the balls as he banged away at them. He worked off an emotion and might just have improved his game in the process.

(5) Keep short accounts with your family. If there

is an explosion, patch it up as soon as possible. Don't let it drag on for days with the whole household under an emotional cloud. Every family should adopt the principle, "Let not the sun go down on your wrath."

(6) Try a decisive motivational action. Remember the saying, "It is much easier to act yourself into a new way of feeling than to feel yourself into a new way of acting." Act, then feel. If you don't feel it, deliberately break the cycle; square your shoulders, put a smile on your face, and move toward people.

(7) Clarify your communication. An emotional short-circuit is conveying a message, but it is distorted and indistinct and open to a variety of interpretations. Communicate verbally. Put your message into words.

(8) Try stopping the emotional reaction before it starts. Deny yourself the luxury of an emotional debauch. Take seriously the Proverbial approach, "The start of an argument is like the first break in the dam. Stop it before it goes further" (17:14).

TEMPER

Proverbs 3:31	*Proverbs 18:19*
Proverbs 11:29	*Proverbs 19:11*
Proverbs 12:16	*Proverbs 19:12*
Proverbs 13:3	*Proverbs 20:2*
Proverbs 14:29	*Proverbs 25:23*
Proverbs 15:18	*Proverbs 25:28*
Proverbs 16:14	*Proverbs 27:4*
Proverbs 16:32	*Proverbs 29:11*
Proverbs 17:14	*Proverbs 29:20*

Proverbs 30:33

8

A TALE OF TWO SONS—ONE PROVERBIAL, ONE PERVERSE

In one sense Proverbs may be said to be the book of father-son relationship, with the first seven chapters given over to admonitions of a father to his son. The expression, "to my son," is constantly repeated throughout the book as the wise, experienced father constantly warns his son about many of the dangers he will face. In one most intimate verse Solomon says, "For I, too, was once a son, tenderly loved by my mother as an only child, and the companion of my father" (4:3), and in a moment we are ushered into the family of David, Solomon's father.

King David was remarkable in many ways. He started in the modest occupation of tending sheep on the hillside, and he ultimately became king of his people. Blessed with unusual gifts of leadership and the capacity to issue a challenge, he was able to call forth a response from his followers, who left hearth and home to join his band of roving men. David's mighty men, living in the mountains under the contagion of his personal magnetism, wrote a new and illustrious page in Israel's history.

As he listened to the song of the bird, the rustling wind, and the babbling brook, the shepherd boy took his harp and strummed his songs until he became known as "the sweet singer of Israel." The book of Psalms contains many of his songs that stir the whole gamut of emotions— from the depth of despair in Psalm 31 to the serene confidence of Psalm 23.

Because of his clear, spiritual perception, David came to be known as "a man after God's own heart." At his worst he was rough, sensual, earthy; at his best, a great saint from whose pen spiritual precepts flowed that have been a continuing source of inspiration across the centuries. A remarkable statesman, he took a poor, dispirited little kingdom and by his direction molded the heterogeneous elements into a compact and unified nation.

It could be said David's life was a great success story. He was a success as a leader, poet, singer, king, and man of spiritual insight, but when it came to rearing children he had mixed results.

The problems of father-son relationships are clearly seen in David's two sons, Solomon and Absalom. The two boys are a study in contrasts as they trod two different pathways in life. Absalom, the suave, sophisticated playboy who spent money with a lavish hand and enjoyed the adulation of the crowd, stirring up strife and revolt. Solomon, studious and thoughtful, giving himself to the studies of *flora* and *fauna,* composing songs and collecting proverbs destined to lead Israel to its largest era of peace.

THE IMPORTANCE OF A FATHER FIGURE

"A father punishes a son he delights in" (3:11). In the days of David there was no doubt about the role of the father in the home. The man was in full and complete control. Some of the experiences recorded in David's life form a sad commentary on the status of women in that day, when men had the all-important position in society. In modern times a somewhat different situation has developed.

Some observers have characterized it as "the effeminization of American society." Sociologists have speculated that while the men were out on the frontier endeavoring to tame the wilderness and carve out a new empire, it was inevitable that women should be left at home to care for the family.

In many foreign cultures there is no doubt that the husband is in charge of the household, the wife and children being in a subservient position. But in the US things are different. A favorite story on one Air Force base tells about an attentive Japanese wife who waited hand and foot upon her American husband. She shocked the American wives by her devotion and attention to him. On the day that she received her United States citizenship her husband sank into his easy chair and as usual called for his slippers. She confounded him by replying, "I'm an American citizen now. Get them yourself!"

In the middle class, which comprises a very important section of American culture, wives tend to be in charge of the family affairs. The husbands are not nearly so important. The father goes out to earn the living and is often away from early morning until late at night, so responsibility for the family falls upon the mother. She is the chauffeur, the disciplinarian, the arbitrator in fights and discussions, the housekeeper, and the bill payer.

A man growing up in our American culture may spend all of his days under the care of a woman. He has a woman for a mother. As soon as he is old enough, it may be that she will go off to work and leave him under the care of another woman who is his baby-sitter. At school he discovers one of the anomalies of our American educational system—that a great portion of the teachers are women. So a growing schoolboy may remain constantly under the supervision of a woman. The youngster at last finishes high school. It could be that he might be exposed to a masculine figure in college, but he then looks around for some woman whom he can marry so that she will be able to watch over him, care for him, perhaps even put him through college, and then share the rest of his days with him. Thus, the overshadowing female may be a constant support to the frail male through all the days of his earthly pilgrimage.

When I first began my work as a minister I went out to a small mountain town to start a new church. I had been converted only about eight months. How did I know how to establish and run a church? I thought about the minister of the church from which I came. Reverend Marks wore a gray suit, I wore a gray suit; he wore a black tie, I wore a black tie; he carried a New Testament in his hip pocket, I carried one in mine. Whatever I was doing I asked myself, "How would Reverend Marks do it?" Psychologists would say Reverend Marks was my model. How does a boy grow to be a man? He looks for a model. Who is the most obvious model? The close-at-hand father figure.

Social-science investigators have been calling attention to the importance of the masculine figure in a developing boy's life. The Korean War jolted American complacency with the news that for the first time in American history twenty-one GI's had elected to stay in enemy hands. Virginia Paisley investigated their backgrounds and found that out of twenty-one, nineteen of them felt unwanted by their fathers or stepfathers. She further discovered that eleven lost their fathers at an early age, either by divorce or by death. Obviously, these boys had personality defects which came, in part at least, from lack of an adequate father figure in their lives.

Similarly, with girls there are indications of the need for a strong masculine figure in their lives. Father is a symbol of what men are like (masculinity). He is the representative head of the family—often the breadwinner and economic provider. He is the symbol of authority. She sees in him the image of the lover-husband with whom one day she will share her life.

An issue of a magazine carried an article entitled "The Search for a Phantom Father," which discussed the tragedy of office romances of girls in the twenty-five or thirty-five year age bracket who became involved with males many years their senior. The men never intended to desert their wives and from the girls' viewpoint the future of such a romance was very bleak. Nevertheless, some girls risked everything for their romantic fling. From his investigations the writer concluded that one reason for the romances was an unsatisfactory father figure. The girls' fathers had often been a "Caspar Milquetoast" or were in some other way unsatisfactory. Now, they were really searching for a father. It was indeed "the search for a phantom father."

Sociologists have also been pointing out the importance of father figures. Sheldon and Eleanor Glueck, in their book *Predicting Delinquency and Crime,* have set up a fivefold criteria with which it is possible to predict with considerable accuracy the future criminal career or experience of delinquency of a child. Of the five factors involved in predicting what was going to happen in the lives of children, two have to do with the father—his discipline and his relationship with his son.

In an investigation carried out at a large seminary with leaders in religious education, an effort was made to discover how important father figures were in the lives of these people. It was discovered that successful leaders had almost invariably come from homes where there were good father figures. Unsuccessful leaders had just as invariably been associated with homes where there were unsatisfactory father figures.

Far more important than all of the foregoing is the discovery by psychologists that there is a tendency for the child to make God in its father's image. In a Christian counseling center it was found that in many cases of problems concerning religious faith there was some type of parental difficulty in the background with the father more significant than the mother. If the father was cruel and repressive, God was feared and resented. In cases where the father was casual and negligent, the child tended to be indifferent to God. Where the father was inconsistent in his discipline, the individual found it difficult to ever trust God.

All of this is saying that whether we look at it psychologically, sociologically, or from the purely religious point of view, the father is of vital importance in the developing life of the child.

THE PROVERBIAL SON

"For I, too, was once a son, tenderly loved by my mother as an only child, and the companion of my father" (4:3).

Solomon apparently occupied a special place in the affections of his father. He was the son of Bathsheba, the woman who had brought David the moments of his greatest degradation. She had been the wife of Uriah the Hittite, whom David had caused to be sent to certain death in battle. Following that death David took Bathsheba as his wife. The first child born of that union died. That, along with the confrontation of Nathan the prophet, brought to pass the lowest point in David's varied life. Solomon's birth apparently brought the king much joy.

Bathsheba was David's favorite wife, and the note of love and affection between a man and a wife found so often in the book of Proverbs is probably a reflection of the good relationship they enjoyed. "The man who finds a wife finds a good thing, she is a blessing to him from the Lord" (18:22). The message of a father-mother relationship is constantly found in this book. "Happy is the man with a levelheaded son; sad the mother of a rebel" (10:1). "Listen to your father and mother. What you learn from them will stand you in good stead" (1:8). This emphasis on a good father-and-mother love relationship is badly needed today. Children need to see manifestations of love in the basic relationships between their fathers and mothers. One man put it well when he said, "I love my children best when I love their mother." This basic love relationship provides a foundation upon which all the other love relationships in the family can be built.

THE PERVERSE SON

"A rebellious son is a grief to his father and a bitter blow to his mother" (17:25).

Possibly the saddest words that ever fell from David's lips were uttered in reference to Absalom. A messenger had brought him the news of Absalom's death, and the Bible says, "The king was much moved, and went up to the chamber over the gate and wept: and as he went, thus he said, O my son Absalom, my son, my son Absalom! would God I had died for thee, O Absalom, my son, my son!" (2 Sam. 18:33, KJV).

David had failed, and many factors went into this failure. David missed his opportunity with his son Absalom. In most areas of life it is possible to make a mistake and later on return to try again. But in an experience of rearing children it is not possible to go back and start over again. A youth cannot go back and become a child. He must, of necessity, continue to grow. Psychologists speak of the "teachable moment." There is a certain moment in experience when an individual is ready to learn a lesson. If he does not learn the lesson at this particular time, in all probability he will never learn it at all, and future development may be unsatisfactory. Shakespeare said it in *Julius Caesar:*

> *There is a tide in the affairs of men,*
> *Which, taken at the flood, leads on to fortune;*
> *Omitted, all the voyage of their life*
> *Is bound in shallows and in miseries.*

If a father's role is not fulfilled at the appropriate time in the developing child's life, his great opportunity will have been missed. As Esau found no place for repentance, so with us; there may be no chance to go back and undo the past.

David shifted the responsibility for looking after his son. As he dealt with his son he gave the task of relaying messages to other people, using intermediaries and expecting them to accept responsibility for looking after him. In the last tragic episode of his experience he requested the officers going off to war to "deal gently with the young man." Naturally, these men made an independent judgment and when they came upon Absalom, hanging from a tree by his raven locks, thrust in the vengeful spear. Someone has said that Absalom never went to his father with a broken toy; consequently he never went to him with a broken heart.

A study carried out in a seminary discovered that in the experience of religious awakening there were four influential figures—the mother, the minister, the father, and the Sunday School teacher. It is a sad commentary upon the influence of a father that he should have had less influence in the spiritual experience of his child than did the minister. The time has come when the responsibility for the character development of the children must be fairly and squarely laid at the feet of each father.

David was busy about many important things—leading a people, ruling a nation, writing beautiful poetry. Was this busyness really a coverup? Speaking in another connection, a writer has said that busyness is one of the most acceptable escape mechanisms of our day. The important thing is not how much we are doing but with what we are occupied. There are so many men who are busy making a living, piling up money and assets, and forgetting the all-important task of rearing sons and daughters. To paraphrase a challenging Scripture verse, "What shall it profit a man, if he gain the whole world, and lose his own son or daughter?"

David set a bad example for Absalom. He became a prodigal in the darkest moment of his life and murdered a man in an effort to cover his misdemeanor. Later, he became a great saint. God forgave him and welcomed him back. David came to be spoken of by the inspired writer as a man after God's own heart. Gifted with spiritual insight, through his writings he ministered to the generations yet to be, but his saintly living never brought Absalom, who had followed him into the far country, back into contact with God. Although David came back, Absalom didn't bother to come with him. The example a father leaves before his child will always be one of the most telling and vital things that he ever does.

THE ENRICHMENT OF THE FATHERHOOD CONCEPT

"Young man, do not resent it when God chastens and corrects you, for his punishment is proof of his love. Just as a father punishes a son he delights in to make him better, so the Lord corrects you" (3:11–12).
Right through the Old Testament there is a constant concern for the "fatherless" and there are many exhortations to the Jewish people to accept responsibility for caring for those left without fathers. Experiments by psychologists have shown that substitute parents are often very good. It is not the biological fact of fatherhood, but the emotional relationship that comes to exist between a man and a child.

Since many fathers will not accept the responsibility for their children, Christian men often have to step out and become substitute fathers, as they work with boys in the organizational life of the church.

Unfortunately, many men do not think about their responsibility of being adequate fathers. I once addressed a dads' club in an influential area of the city. After the meeting was over, one of the officers thanked me for the talk and said that in all his years of attending the dads' club this was the first time anyone had ever spoken on the importance of being a good father. Surely it is not illogical for a dads' club to occasionally consider the subject of fatherhood—it might get a mention.

In biblical times great responsibility was placed on the fathers' shoulders, but we have all too easily shrugged it off. Many marriage counselors feel that women are much more ready than men are to study child psychology. We must take time to learn the art of fatherhood, just as we do to learn any other skill.

Some of David's greatest writings came from his most bitter experiences. It might well be that Psalm 103, traditionally described as "a psalm of David," sprang from his spiritual insights at the news of Absalom's death. One of David's most definitive writings about the nature of God, this psalm contrasts the frailties of man with the grandeur and greatness of God. Despite the magnitude of God, David asserts and reasserts his patience and mercy in the glad assurance that, "As far as the east is from the west, so far hath he removed our transgressions from us." In the central verse of the psalm he states his overall theme, "Like as a father pitieth his children, so the Lord pitieth them that fear him."

In the Bible the term "Father" is a favored one for describing God. Perhaps the most graphic story Jesus ever told was of the son's going into the far country and of the father's waiting for him to come back home again. Jesus frequently reminded his followers of the relationship between God and his children. He told them that God would watch over them far more carefully than any earthly father would. In the Model Prayer, Jesus taught people to say, "Our Father which art in heaven." Here we see the idealized fatherhood, which represents fatherhood at its highest, in the wonder of the love of God for men and women.

This Father who is in heaven wants a relationship with his children, and such a relationship can only come when an individual has an experience of faith in Christ, and consequently becomes a child of God. The relationship is made possible by the death of Christ upon the cross. Through this, God invites people to have the experience of the new birth and become children of the living God.

"Bleak House," one of Charles Dickens' most moving stories, tells of Jo, the crossing sweeper. Jo worked at his humble task, sweeping the crossing and hoping for the pennies which people would throw to him. On one occasion he was asked about his father and mother. His response was, "I neber knowed nothing about 'em." Later in the story Jo was ill, lying in a dismal attic room. He was attended by a kind Christian doctor, Allan Woodcourt.

The doctor spoke to the sinking boy and asked, "Do you hear me, Jo?"

Jo responded, "I hear you, sir. It's dark, but I'm a-groping, I'm a-groping. Let me catch hold of your hand."

Dr. Woodcourt said, "Can you say what I say?"

Jo responded, "I'll say anything you say, for I know it is good."

The doctor said, "Our Father which art in heaven."

Jo replied, "Yes, that's wery good, sir, wery good," and with that, Jo, who "neber knowed nothing" about his father or mother, entered into the most wonderful of all relationships as he passed into the presence of his heavenly Father.

As vital as fatherhood is and as significant as the father figure is in the life of the growing individual in the family unit, it is important that fathers be at their best. No man can ever be at his best without a right relationship with God. Above everything else, he who is to be an adequate father must have God as his Father.

THE PROVERBIAL FATHER-SON RELATIONSHIP

Proverbs 1:8   *Proverbs 10:1*
Proverbs 1:10   *Proverbs 13:24*
Proverbs 3:11   *Proverbs 17:25*
Proverbs 4:3   *Proverbs 19:13*
Proverbs 23:26

9

COMMUNICATION IN THE PROVERBIAL FAMILY

Solomon would never forget that day. It had started in the early morning as he stood at his father's side watching the three army groups led by Joab, Abishai, and Ittai preparing to move out on the search-and-destroy mission aimed at subduing the revolution being fomented by the rebellious Absalom.

David had wanted to go himself and seek a confrontation with his recalcitrant son, but his advisors, aware of the overwhelming difficulties of a father-son encounter, had counseled against it. They urged the king to remain in the capital to await the outcome of the conflict. With a heavy heart David bade farewell to the assembled units of the army and gave his final command, "Deal gently, for my sake, with the young man, Absalom."

All day David and Solomon had waited for the news from the two armies they knew to be locked in conflict. As the battle waxed and waned, David's forces had rallied for a great effort and finally driven Absalom's army fleeing before the king's forces in defeat. Absalom himself, seeking to escape, had ignominiously mounted a mule and ridden off, but as he urged the beast on through the forest his magnificent head of hair was suddenly snagged in the boughs of a great oak tree, yanking him from the animal's back and leaving him hanging and swinging like some great pendulum.

Joab, smelling the scent of victory, came racing up and paused only for a moment to savor the sight of the rebellious prince completely helpless and writhing in frustrated rage. Contrary to David's plea to grant mercy, Joab plunged in three spears, the prelude to a hail of barbs from his followers.

Sitting on the wall of the city alongside the gates, David scanned the horizon and hoped for news. He jumped anxiously to his feet as the watchman called to announce two messengers approaching, one at a considerable distance behind the other.

Ahimaaz came stumbling in through the gates to announce victory. The king's forces had triumphed. But David had another matter on his heart, "Is the young man Absalom safe?" Ahimaaz couldn't or wouldn't answer the king's question, and muttered that the scene was confused, he didn't know the particulars.

Then came Cushai, the second runner, who brought the dreaded news of Absalom's death.

The memory of those two messengers—one confused, the other clear—long remained with Solomon. In his later writings he tried, not only to make his own messages clear and precise, but also to exhort his readers to take trouble with their own communications.

THE MISUSE OF WORDS

"Some people like to make cutting remarks, but the words of the wise soothe and heal" (12:18).

Amid the colorful stories of the Old Testament none is

more fascinating for the student of communication than that of a peculiar situation following a battle between the men of Gilead and the Ephraimites.

Jephthah, leader of the Gileadites, had bottled up the Ephraimites and gained control of the Jordan River crossings that provided the only way of escape. His problem was to distinguish friend from foe as they forded the river. He discovered a simple answer in the speech peculiarity of the Ephraimites who were unable to enunciate the *sh* sound.

As each man came across the ford, claiming he was a Gileadite, he was asked to repeat *shibboleth*, the Hebrew word for corn. If the fugitive responded with *shibboleth*, he was immediately recognized as an Ephraimite.

The dictionary today defines the word *shibboleth* as a "password," but this entails a misunderstanding of the original incident. The importance lay not in the word as a word but rather the way in which the word was pronounced. It was not a test of knowledge of a particular word but a check of the individual's capacity to enunciate correctly.

The mode of expression always plays a vital role in communication.

I have had some bad experiences with dining in fancy eating places where ordering by the menu descriptions is a hazardous process I like to dub "restaurant roulette." I read, "fluffy golden omelette made from three country-fresh grade AA eggs." Then comes a flat, sorry-looking, greasy lump of yellow which makes me want to ask, "Is that a fluffy, golden omelette?"

It seemed that a certain cafeteria was the answer to my problem. The food is top quality. I see it displayed, and I can be selective, putting together the sort of meal that will satisfy my appetite, conform to my diet, and fit my budget.

A certain cafeteria certainly knows how to display its food, coordinating the colors, cleverly arranging the dishes, garnishing the borders, decorating fruits—just the right lighting. Behind each of these islands of gastronomic delight stands a presiding assistant neatly clad in black dress with just the right relief of white apron and collar. And herein is my problem. The assistant is the serpent in this Eden of luscious food.

The high priestess of the vegetable section is a nice-looking, middle-aged woman whose face has set into a sort of sneer. As a patron approaches, she says with her mouth, "Can I help you?" Before she is finished placing the meager piece of broccoli on his plate, she intones, "What else, please? But the automatic, bored manner of address and the tone of her voice say, "For goodness sake, hurry on," while the pained look on her face fairly shouts, "Only one vegetable—what a cheapskate."

The communication problem here is that, though the message coming from the brain may be successfully put into words, the way it is transmitted determines whether or not the message will be received.

Joseph Conrad, skillful craftsman of literature and wizard in the use of words, is credited with saying, "Give me the right word and the right accent, and I will move the world." Communication does not exist in words alone. The manner in which the message is transmitted can make all the difference between its being a "cutting remark" and a word that "soothes and heals."

There's a good chance the lady in the cafeteria may be particularly competent because she has been practicing at home. Husbands and wives are frequently past masters of the art of using a polite, courteous term to convey something less than a courteous message.

It takes practice for a married person to learn to address his spouse as "hon——eee," "darl——ing," or "sweet—hear—r—rt" in such a way as to bring out the last syllable like the crack of a whip. In this way the term of endearment will carry a rebuke to a spouse. The language of love literally drips with venom.

A popular literary device is the use of irony—a statement which says one thing on the surface but underneath means exactly the opposite. While irony may have a gentle, teasing overtone, it may also bite, and the speaker transmits sarcasm by verbal expression.

Mr. Solomon, a hard-working accountant, sits looking over the report card brought home from school by his son Jimmy. His offspring, at this moment vividly aware of his poor showing, apprehensively awaits the paternal reaction. His father's words are laudatory: "You certainly make a father proud of his son." But the manner of expression tells the boy his father is disappointed and upset.

Husbands and wives often become experts in the art of verbal cut and nick called sarcasm. Mr. Taylor, gazing at the TV dinner just placed before him by his spouse, remarks, "You've obviously been taking a course in gourmet cooking."

Mrs. Briggs, who's been fussing at her husband for spending so much time playing poker, looks at the bonus check brought home by her spouse: "That's some bonus check, Harry."

A husband, aware of his wife's bridge-playing activities stands looking over the den: "I've gotta give it to you, Vera, you're a tremendous housekeeper."

Sarcasm is another example of how the manner in which a statement is made changes it. The speaker makes a statement that by itself would have one meaning, but the manner of speech gives it the opposite significance. This method is geared to deliver a rapier thrust or cut and wound the recipient.

Yet another variation of expression is the use of a technique generally called teasing or kidding. In this process the speaker makes a statement obnoxious to his receiver and, after making his point, retreats by saying, "I was only teasing."

Martin Luther's life gave us some beautiful examples of husband-wife relationships. When an artist painted Luther's portrait and wanted to know which was the reformer's best profile, Luther replied, "Paint me, warts and all." This comment typifies Luther's relationship with his wife. The Luthers had a group of students living with them, and these guests recorded verbatim many of the interchanges between Martin and his wife, Katie.

One interchange shows Luther in a teasing mood.

LUTHER: "We shall yet see the day when a man will take several wives."

KATIE: "The devil thinks so."

LUTHER: "The reason, dear Katie, is that a woman can have only one child a year, whereas a man can beget several."

KATIE: "Paul says, 'Let each man have his own wife.'"

LUTHER: "Aye, his own wife, but not only one; that is not in Paul."

Thus the doctor joked a long time until Katie said: "Before I would stand for that, I would go back to the convent and leave you and all your children!" Luther, who would fight to the death for the principle of monogamy, enjoyed teasing his wife about the alleged masculine bent toward polygamy.

Many teasers have a more specific goal in mind and will test the situation by pushing things as far as they can before retreating. Teasing can develop into a subtle torture carried on in public and causing the recipient intense, silent agony. When the victim finally turns, the adept teaser laughs it off with, "I was only teasing." Teasing stands with

sarcasm as one of the cruelest uses of communication. As
Proverbs suggests it, "A man who is caught lying to his
neighbor and says, 'I was just fooling,' is like a madman
throwing around firebrands, arrows and death!" (26:18–
19).

DO YOU HAVE YOUR EARS ON?

"If you profit from constructive criticism you will
be elected to the wise men's hall of fame. But to reject
criticism is to harm yourself and your own best interests"
(15:31–32).
Citizens Band radios have brought a new day in communication and opened the possibilities of people getting in touch
with each other. One of the favorite expressions of the
CB'er trying to contact another person in a nearby vehicle
is to ask, "Do you have your hears on?"—reminding us
that communication is a two-way street, and receiving is
just as important as transmitting in any communication
experience. Proverbs emphasizes the receiving aspect of
communication by exhorting the reader to be willing to
receive feedback.

Equally picturesque in the esoteric world of CB are
the "handles" or pseudonyms used by CB'ers. "Dirty Bird"
and "Blue Goose" are two normally peaceful residents in a
large southwestern city. These two gentlemen apparently
had little in common beyond their affinity in using "handles"
associated with the world of ornithology, but they demonstrated at least one of the problems of communication.
"Dirty Bird" was trying frantically to get the use of Channel
19, but Blue Goose was just as sure he had airways and
wasn't going to give it up and refused to listen to Blue
Goose's pleas. In the unfortunate altercation which followed both men pulled weapons and killed each other!
While in no way prophesying that refusing feedback will
likely lead to homicide, it is vastly important that we be
aware of the benefits feedback can bring us.

A very attractive young lady in a counseling center related her concern about her relationships with men. Because of her good looks and modish dress she had little trouble in getting a man's attention, and dates came thick and fast. But after a brief, intense experience a man would suddenly lose interest in her. As she was now in her late twenties, she had high hopes of marriage, and each of these experiences devastated her, leaving her with a feeling of being exploited.

As she told her story, she broke down and cried. The counselor asked why she did this, and she responded in a coquettish manner, "I thought you men liked women who broke down and sought a big shoulder to cry on." It turned out she thought this was the way she could make herself more attractive to the male. The counselor was able to point out that he was not impressed with her tears. In fact, she came across as a weepy, drooping gal and became an object of pity rather than the attractive person she should be. She desperately needed the feedback experience the counselor provided.

Not everyone who needs feedback is willing to accept what he is told. While being insensitive to the effects of his behavior on other people, he can become excessively sensitive to information given to him and respond by becoming angry, crying, threatening to leave, or refusing to talk. Whereas the ideal stance in encouraging feedback is to listen, he may become very expressive, believing that attack is the best means of defense.

The famous Scottish poet expressed what most of us intuitively know.

> O wad some Power the giftie gie us
> To see oursels as ithers see us!
> It was frae monie a blunder free us . . .

We all need feedback. The most difficult of all feedback for us to accept is the so-called negative feedback or criticism. Here are some suggestions about the best attitude towards negative feedback.

Nine principles to use in accepting criticism:

(1) Be quiet while you are being criticized and make clear that you are listening.

(2) Look directly at the person talking to you.

(3) Under no condition find fault with the person who has just criticized you.

(4) Don't create the impression that the other person is destroying your spirit.

(5) Don't jest.

(6) Don't caricature the complaint.

(7) Don't change the subject.

(8) Don't imply that your critic has some ulterior, hostile motive.

(9) Convey to the other person that you understand his objection.

Take a positive attitude towards criticism. Remember many people in different walks of life pay teachers, coaches and critics to help them with criticism of their particular activities. Proverbs is particularly long on the value of you accepting criticism. "If you refuse criticism you will end in poverty and disgrace; if you accept criticism you are on the road to fame" (13:18).

RESPONDING TO POSITIVE FEEDBACK

The last chapter of Proverbs reports an experience between a husband and wife and tells about how this husband praises his wife by saying, "There are many fine women in the world, but you are the best of them all!" (31:29).

How did this woman respond? We don't know, but from experience I can say it is often more difficult for a person to react to positive feedback than it is to criticism. Here are some principles which may help.

(1) Don't feel compelled to "trade." While it certainly is desirable that you should be ready to return a compliment, to give indication that you are not so self-centered that you do not see something of value in the person who is complimenting you, it is not an absolute necessity. You can accept the compliment in the sincere spirit in which it is offered and say, "Thank you."

(2) Don't deny the statement. There's nothing more devastating than to pass on a compliment to someone and have them refuse it. It's rather like feeding an animal that bites your hand. Gary Nelson took this attitude. As he sat in groups one evening and lamented his lack of ability, he happened to mention he'd bought a stereo kit and put it together. The men in the group all expressed an interest, so the following week Gary turned up with the completed unit in a large box. Harry Gordon, who had the reputation as an experienced radio ham, said, "That's an excellent job. I can see you've put in a lot of time on it." Gary replied, "Oh, come on, be honest. It's amateurish, and you know it."

Gary had embarrassed Harry who was trying to encourage a newcomer to the field in which he himself had some expertise. How could Gary have responded? One possibility is, "I appreciate a compliment from an expert like you. You encourage me."

(3) Look upon positive feedback as a gesture of goodwill and respond accordingly. The old-fashioned meaning of the word "compliment" was a gift and a present that someone gave to an inferior. Many of us feel it demeans us when someone gives something to us, much the same way as a gratuity might appear to a servant. Let's take a sensible view of ourselves. Don't underrate yourself. You have certain special gifts and because of these you are entitled to appropriate appreciation.

(4) Don't question the motives of the person who gives you positive feedback. In the sort of competitive society within which we live we are all too used to people softening us up before trying to get something from us. From a personal experience I know when someone compliments me; especially if he tends to be effusive, I wonder if he has an ulterior motive. Is he setting me up to make a sale? But he may be a person of good will who is sincerely trying to encourage me in something I am undertaking. I should accept his compliment at face value and not have some paranoid suspicion that he is trying to get to me.

(5) Don't let the fear of criticism deny you the right of positive feedback. One of the best techniques of criticism is to find something to commend before you criticize. We have all had contact with people who use the technique of paving the way for criticism by complimenting, "This is very good, but . . ." So when we hear a compliment we may steel ourselves. But the person giving us positive feedback may have had no idea at all of being critical. Don't rush out to meet criticism halfway.

(6) Don't be too naïve. Some people like to give a compliment. I once had a cute little co-ed in one of my classes. She would come up after every class with a beaming smile and excitedly verbalize, "Oh, that was so wonderful. Your lectures are so marvelous." I hope they were marvelous to her—but I'm realist enough to know my utterances aren't always inspired; in fact, some of them are very mediocre. Robert Montgomery, referring to applause said, "Enjoy it, but never quite believe it." Make a realistic evaluation of yourself.

THE RIGHT WORD AT THE RIGHT TIME

"Everyone enjoys giving good advice, and how wonderful it is to be able to say the right thing at the right time" (15:23).

Having considered the difficulties we encounter in receiving criticism, we can more readily understand the delicate task family members face when they try to help other family members correct some area of deficiency in their lives. It seems as if we become particularly sensitive to people who live close to us. It is easier to take criticism from someone outside the family than a fellow family member, so it becomes increasing important that we learn techniques of criticizing effectively.

Most of us believe in "constructive criticism," but the way we interpret this phrase depends on our perspective. If you are offering criticism, you are aware of your altruistic ideals and how you may be able to help another person develop his potential. The word *constructive* is pre-eminent in your mind.

However, if you are on the receiving end, the word *criticism* leaps out at you in letters of fire, and your self-love is offended. You see your critic as a self-righteous individual who never looks at himself but who, from his ivory tower of self-satisfaction, spends his time searching out the faults of others. You are immediately beset with the temptation to make a reflex response by reversing the situation and criticizing him rather than fairly evaluating what has been suggested to you.

Yet criticism must be given. Coaching any sport, teaching any skill, training in any area is dependent upon some type of criticism by an onlooker. Learn the skill of tactfully offering criticism, and you can count it a major achievement.

Sugar-coat the pill of criticism. Unlike the tennis player who is paying ten dollars per hour and is most grateful for the suggestions the coach gives him, most people feel that criticism is a blow to their self-love. Because praise is the greatest reward we can give another person, the best way to criticize is by offering praise first. In *Julius Caesar,*

Shakespeare depicts Mark Anthony as a man vividly aware of the importance of praise before criticism. He's out to get Brutus's scalp. Nevertheless, he leads off by saying, "For Brutus is an honorable man; So are they all, all honorable men." As he moves along, this clever speaker is able to turn tables on his enemies, arouse the mob, and achieve his original purpose.

Suppose you are worried about your wife's lack of punctuality and feel the time has come to say something. But you are concerned because your spouse frequently interprets your efforts to pass on information as "attacking" her. How do you go about this?

You could lead off with, "Honey, I want you to know how much I appreciate the way you keep house. I'm always proud when we have guests. I'm grateful for the way you work your fingers to the bone looking after the children and for your sweet spirit in all that you do. It may be I'm a bit finicky about things, but I would sure appreciate it if you could be ready when it's time for us to leave. It bugs me when I'm late."

You have gotten your message across to your wife, but you've put a nice sugar-coating on it by paying her a series of compliments and acknowledging that you might be a little finicky.

Begin with yourself. One of the main benefits of participating in group therapy is the process of feedback. In such a situation the other members tell a person about some aspects of his personality that could be improved.

As practical as this procedure would appear to be, in actual practice there are some problems. It depends mainly on the manner in which the criticizer goes about his work.

In our counseling center we use a type of group therapy called Integrity Therapy. The leaders have developed a way of dealing with the problem of criticism. A group member is told, "If you wish to tell someone else what to do in a given situation, you must 'earn the right' by talking about your own failures before telling anyone else about his failures."

We have discovered that when this technique is used, few people are ever upset by someone in the group "putting them right." Once the person has spoken of his own failures, he establishes his position as an equal, rather than a superior. From this perspective, his criticism is acceptable.

In a counseling interview Mrs. Nordan told me a moving story of communication problems with her eighteen-year-old daughter. Julia, in college, was "goofing off" and failing in her courses. She called her mother and confessed that she had been missing classes and would shortly be in difficulty with the university authorities.

Mrs. Nordan in her frustration asked, "What can I do?"

I asked if she as an adolescent had ever "goofed off." The troubled mother sat and thought, then responded, "I certainly did. Do I have to tell you?"

"No. Not me. Why not try telling your daughter?"

Mrs. Nordan had always started discussions with her daughter by saying, "When I was a girl, I . . ." and then proceeded to tell Julia about her industry and diligence, providing a list of mother's adolescent virtues. She approached Julia from her strengths! I suggested she reverse her procedure and tell Julia about her own failures in adolescence.

When Mrs. Nordan returned, she came with a smiling face. Mrs. Nordan confessed her adolescent failures; her daughter then had broken down to talk of her irresponsibilities and indiscretions.

"Begin with yourself" might well be the motto of any successful critic.

Give your subject a chance to save his face. If the aim of criticism is to help the individual change some facet of his life, it is a good idea to give him an "out."

A friend of mine is a professor who has large classes in a required introductory course. Many of his students are not overly enthusiastic, and some use the time in class to catch up on their reading for other courses.

From his elevated platform the professor can see far more than the students ever imagine. When he sees a student reading, it bugs him no end, but he has learned to maintain a calm outward appearance.

The professor addresses his class, "I may be wrong, but I've got an idea that a student is reading a book that has no connection with this course. As I said, I may be mistaken, but if it is the case, I will certainly have it in mind when I prepare the grades for the members of this class."

The professor has served a notice of warning on the transgressor who generally manages to do something about the situation. Nevertheless, this professor has also provided the individual with an out by saying, "I may be mistaken."

Statements like, "I could be wrong," "Perhaps I am looking at it the wrong way," "I may not have made the situation clear at the beginning," "Perhaps I should have explained things and not left it open for misinterpretation," all help to provide the individual with a way by which he can change and not feel too badly about it.

Issue a courteous challenge. There are times when someone in your family must be told to change a procedure, and there is very little to commend and not much sense in the critic's speaking of his own failures.

A pastor of a large church had managed to persuade his congregation to buy time on television. Wanting to make maximum use of this video time, he sought the aid of a television consultant. The expert suggested they present their program in its normal format. After the presentation the consultant spoke to the minister of music who had planned and performed on the program. The consultant said, "Are you thin-skinned? Can you take criticism?"

The minister of music replied that he wanted help from the expert. Whereupon the visitor said, "I don't think you ought to sing solos on television."

How I wish this courageous man would talk with some singers I know. Think of how much suffering many of us would be saved!

The secret lay in the challenge, "Are you thin-skinned? Can you take criticism?"

The way a method expression makes a message more palatable was demonstrated by the techniques of a gifted psychotherapist who worked in therapy groups and used confrontational methods. He masked his incisive mind behind an engaging smile. As the session progressed, the time came for him to do some confronting, and he launched into the process of facing a group member with some negative aspect of his adjustment to life.

The therapist turned his beaming countenance upon the subject and, in a voice sounding for all the world like a fond parent expressing loving disappointment, made the frankest statements: "That certainly was a childish action to take." "You have obviously been very irresponsible." "You didn't show up too well there." All of this he did with his face wreathed in a winning smile. Very seldom did anybody take umbrage at the statements which normally would have made them hopping mad. The expression on his face and the note of concern in his voice made all the difference in communicating the message.

In the give-and-take of the communication process, few areas will ever be as difficult as giving criticism, but few will have as much possibility for helping other people achieve their potential.

PROVERBIAL TEACHINGS ON COMMUNICATION AND CRITICISM

Proverbs 12:17–19	*Proverbs 18:21*
Proverbs 13:17	*Proverbs 23:12*
Proverbs 13:18	*Proverbs 25:11*
Proverbs 15:12	*Proverbs 25:12*
Proverbs 15:23	*Proverbs 26:18–19*
Proverbs 15:31–32	*Proverbs 26:20–21*
Proverbs 16:23–24	*Proverbs 29:1*

Proverbs 29:5–6

10

THE WISDOM OF
LISTENING

Listen and grow wise. Proverbs 4:1

Mrs. Spencer told her counselor: "My husband and I have problems in talking to each other."

Mr. Spencer, until this moment rather passive, looked startled—then reacted, "I don't believe that's the problem. We both do plenty of talking. The trouble is, we don't bother to listen to each other."

One perceptive psychologist undertook a study of the conversational activities of males and females eating in restaurants. Looking over these masculine-feminine diads she sought to conclude whether the participants were married or unmarried. As time went on, she developed a remarkable skill, and claimed she had attained a 90 percent accuracy in her predictions. Her method was the essence of simplicity. She surveyed the couples at the tables in the restaurant. If they were looking into each other's eyes, hanging to their partner's every word, giving undivided attention—they were probably unmarried.

If, on the other hand, they looked rather like a couple of strangers the maitre d' had been compelled to seat at the same table because of space problems, or they sat in silence while they worked their way through the food—

giving all their attention to whatever they were eating—
there was a good chance they were married.

Listening, this all-important aspect of communication known as the assimilative communication skill, may
give us a clue to many of the problems of human relations
in general and marriage family relationships in particular.
Listening is an area in which the Proverbs has much to say.

THE PRIMACY OF LISTENING

"Listen to me, my son! I know what I am saying.
Listen" (5:1).

Mr. Henry was in a towering rage. Before he departed on
his most recent business trip, he'd given his son, Ted, a
long lecture on the importance of watering his prize orchids.
As he'd given the instructions, Mr. Henry was vaguely
aware of Ted's casual attitude and easy countenance which
said in effect, "Sure, Pop, just leave it to me."

On his return Mr. Henry hurried out to the greenhouse and found his precious plants in a wilted condition,
giving evidence of Ted's neglect. The older Henry proceeded to pour out his wrath on his son who sat, with what
the son felt was commendable patience and tolerance, looking rather like some martyr being persecuted for his faith.

As Mr. Henry noticed the somewhat benign countenance of his son, something within him snapped. Vividly
aware of all his offspring's irresponsibilities and failures, he
yelled, "Do you hear me?"

Of course, the boy heard him; all the household had
heard him; even the neighbors across the street heard him.
The problem was that Ted didn't listen to his father.

Solomon may even have had the same aggravating
experience, and so he said, "Young men, listen to me as
you would to your father. Listen and grow wise, for I
speak the truth—don't turn away" (4:1).

Perhaps the problem is we didn't educate our

children properly in the first place. Our educational processes have given little attention to teaching our children
some all-important verbal communication skills. Teaching
the art of communication has focused primary attention on
the skills of reading and writing. With the growth of com-
pulsory education in most countries this century, the main
drive has been to teach children the three r's, with reading
and writing as the major communication skills, with a
lesser emphasis on speaking. The fourth verbal skill of
listening was virtually ignored.

All of this effort to make people literate has been
no real guarantee they could communicate proficiently. It
has ignored the oral aspects of communication.

Historically, all human communication began as an
oral process of speaking and listening. It continued on this
level for centuries; then, with the invention of the printing
press, the written word came to be considered a prime
means of communication. With the invention and development of radio and television the stress has returned once
more to oral communication.

As far as the family is concerned, oral communication is the major means by which people interact with one
another. Few family members write essays to be read to the
family. Some may write an occasional letter, but it will not
be a particularly lengthy epistle, which the parents discover
when their children go off to college. Even the briefest of
statements on a greeting card seem to represent a monu-
mental effort in written communication between family
members.

The Bible recognizes the primacy of oral communication in teaching the family. The classical passage
concerning the teaching of children is found in the book
of Deuteronomy:

"Hear, O Israel: The Lord our God is one Lord:

"And thou shalt love the Lord thy God with all

thine heart, and with all thy soul, and with all thy might.

"And these words, which I command thee this day, shall be in thine heart!

"And thou shalt teach them diligently unto thy children, and shalt talk of them when thou sittest in thine house, and when thou walkest by the way, and when thou liest down, and when thou risest up" (Deut. 6:4–7, KJV).

The great statement of faith in Deuteronomy is, "The Lord our God is one Lord: And thou shalt love the Lord thy God with all thine heart, and with all thy soul, and with all thy might" (Deut. 6:3, KJV), but it is preceded by the call, "Hear, O Israel."

This note of the importance of listening is carried throughout the Bible. In the New Testament our Lord urged his followers to listen some two hundred times. Ever on his lips were statements such as, "He that hath ears to hear, let him hear" (Matt. 11:15, KJV), and giving his gentle rebuke he asked his followers the question, "Having ears . . . hear ye not?" (Mark 8:18, KJV).

In the light of this emphasis on listening it will be important that we teach our children to be listeners. Parents must set the example so that imitative learning may take place. We begin by acquiring listening skills, no easy task, and then teach these skills to our children.

A TIME FOR SILENCE

"Don't talk so much. You keep putting your foot in your mouth. Be sensible and turn off the flow!" (10:19). If, as some of us believe, the writings of Solomon contain much of the material from a primitive counseling ministry it is appropriate that Solomon in another wisdom book, Ecclesiastes, exhort his listeners to remember, "There is a time to keep silence."

Because communication is more than words and has to do with attitudes and feelings, we suddenly discover the paradoxical situation referred to by the famous psychiatrist Reik, who said of a psychoanalytic session, ". . . what is spoken is not the important thing. It seems to us more important to recognize what speech conceals and what silence reveals." Reik himself has written a book on psychotherapy, *Listening with the Third Ear,* and most trainers of psychotherapists are vividly aware that teaching the aspiring psychotherapist to keep silent is one of the most difficult tasks they face.

A troubled man went to visit his physician with a list of anxieties and fears. The wise doctor told his patient to take a day off and visit the beach. In his hand he placed an envelope and told the man to open it when he reached his destination.

Arriving at the beach he found a quiet spot and opened the envelope. On a small piece of paper he read, "Listen carefully." Recounting the experience later, he told what a rewarding day it was. For the first time in years he heard the lapping of the waves, the song of the bird, and the sighing of the wind. Then he remembered a statement from Carlyle: "Silence is the element in which great things fashion themselves." He discovered that the moment of silence could be the moment of revelation.

All this may give us a clue about the way we can use creative silence to help others. People who master the technique of creative silence say in effect, "I could fill up the time with small talk, and there may even be something I could say which would interest you. But this is not my purpose. I want to provide you with a situation in which you can think about yourself, your failures, shortcomings, problems, assets, and future plans. Because of my interest in you, I am willing to sit in silence with you."

Like any other creative activity, this type of silence calls for self-control and diligent practice. For most of us, ten seconds of silence seems like ten hours of time. The garrulous age in which we live has made us fearful of quietude. Life is too much a carnival of noise when we may really need a chapel of silence.

WORK ON YOUR LEARNING INERTIA

"Listen and grow wise" (4:1).

Although many people may mention that the two words *hearing* and *listening* are synonyms, they are not. Actually they describe two different functions in the communication experience. Hearing describes the activity of a sound wave hitting your ear, and listening is what we call the process of sorting out the auditory stimuli.

The whole operation of a sound wave hitting the ear, and being transmitted to the brain, takes place with lightning speed. The brain itself is programmed by years of experience and conditioning to handle the auditory impressions with which it is fed. Like a busy executive's efficient secretary who sorts out the correspondence, keeping only the most important for his personal perusal, some sounds are summarily rejected, while others have the total attention focused on them.

This selective process carried on by the brain is the main distinction and differences between hearing and listening. From the total number of our auditory impressions we choose a small, select number on which to focus our attention. As the sounds come to us, we hear; when we apply ourselves to their meaning and significance, we listen.

We are living in a day when our environment is not only threatened by air pollution but also by *noise* pollution. Our ears are constantly bombarded by a multiplicity of sounds, and if we paid attention to all these sounds, it would drive us to distraction. So we develop—as a means of self-protection—an internal squelching mechanism by which we automatically reject certain sounds when they come to us. We develop a listening inertia.

Unlike the ground crews of jet airlines who wear ear guards for protection against the ear-splitting sounds of the whining engines, modern man has had to develop a self-protective mechanism to defend himself from the constant acoustical bombardment of twentieth-century living. Most humans are in a lifelong process of gradually building up their own internal ear plugs and training themselves to ignore certain sounds.

I once moved to a house located near a railroad track. For the first few nights every passing train disturbed my sleep. As time went on, I grew to be less and less aware of the noise. One evening a visitor inquired if the passing trains bothered me. I replied, "What trains?" My internal squelching mechanism had taken over so I no longer listened to the railroad noises.

> *"You are an airline pilot flying a four-engine jet from New York to Los Angeles. There are seventy-two people aboard, including nine children, eighteen married couples, twenty-two businessmen, and five crew members. The plane leaves New York at 5:10 P.M. and arrives in Los Angeles six hours and thirty-two minutes later. What was the pilot's name?*
>
> *The first four words give you the answer. However, most people miss it because (1) it is a little bit tricky, and (2) listening is an active task. Most of us are not willing to work at it.*

There is obviously wisdom in the natural tendency we have *not* to listen. The mechanism protects us in many ways, but it also does us a disservice. It causes us to miss many of the things we should listen to. A really observant person has to work hard to overcome what we might call "listening inertia."

All of this means work—hard work—if we are going to get the message that comes to our ears. Or again as Solomon said it, "Don't talk too much. You keep putting

your foot in your mouth. Be sensible and turn off the flow"
(10:19).

LEFTOVER TIME

"Young men, listen to me and never forget what
I'm about to say" (5:7).
One of the problems with listening is that we have time to
spare. While some speakers may verbalize at about 125
words a minute, most of us can think about four times that
speed. As the speaker presents his ideas, we can easily move
along and keep up with him. It is so simple that we have
time on our hands, so we can occasionally dart ahead or go
on a side excursion. These side excursions are particularly
damaging and lead to our downfall as listeners.

As you sit in an audience listening to a speaker, you
may move along with him for a short period. Then a picture of the office flashes onto the screen of your mind, and
you see the work awaiting your attention. So you take a
mental trip back to your place of toil, look over your correspondence, check up on your secretary, and then rejoin
the speaker.

A little later in the discourse the golf course begins
to beckon, and off you go. You bask in the warm sun, ad-
mire the condition of the greens, see the old cronies. Mentally you visualize the beautiful drive, the flawless putt, your
opponent's dismay, and the concluding moment of triumph.

But on one of these side journeys you stay away too
long, and when you return, it is to discover that the speaker
has gotten so far ahead that there is no chance of catching
him. So you sink into a passive resignation to your horrible
fate, put a fixed look on your face, and hope the speaker
will soon tire and quit.

The good listener doesn't go on side excursions. He
tries to anticipate where the speaker is going—gets out
ahead like a scout on a wagon train. As soon as he realizes

the speaker is going in another direction, he hurries back and rejoins him.

CAPTURING THE BALLOONS

"Every young man who listens to me and obeys my instructions will be given wisdom and good sense" (2:1–2). The process of a speaker addressing an audience has been envisaged in a number of ways. One older method was to imagine that each listener had a funnel-like appurtenance fitting on the top of his head. The speaker carried his store of ideas like water in a bucket and conceived his chief task as pouring ideas into the funnel-heads of his auditors.

Because of his distance from the funnel-heads, the speaker was forced to resort to tossing out his buckets of ideas, hoping his aim would be good enough to slosh at least some tiny droplets into the funnels. Thus, the listener was a passive recipient, and the number of ideas he received depended mainly on the throwing ability of the speaker.

A more productive way for the lecturer to see his audience would be to change them from funnel-heads to something more like women sitting in the beauty shop with roller-covered heads. These roller-like contraptions are bumps of knowledge complete with tie-on strings. They are the concepts already possessed by the listeners, and the protruding strings are waiting for familiar thoughts and concepts to be attached.

The communicator on the platform is launching balloons inscribed with messages printed in large letters. Each of his idea-balloons trails a long string, making it a simple matter for the listener to grasp it as it passes by.

While much of the speaker's ability lies in his capacity to adapt his idea-balloons so they match the more obvious tie-down spots on his auditors' heads, the listener is no quiescent squeezed-out sponge. The listener's activity is just as important as the speaker's skill.

A prospective listener sits in an audience. The speaker launches his balloons and sends them floating across the room, trailing their strings. As they sail toward the listener, he is faced with the responsibility for some action and has at least three alternatives.

He may be bodily present but only partly conscious. In his sleepy mistiness he is only vaguely aware of his surroundings. The idea-balloons drift lazily by. For all he knows, they may only be spots before his eyes; so he pays them scant attention, content to relax in the twilight zone of inattentive half-sleep.

Or perhaps the balloons look a little unusual, and for a brief moment he toys with the possibility of closer acquaintance. But they are a trifle strange and bear little relationship to the bumps on his head. After a casual glance he lets them drift on their way.

A third possibility is that the listener may examine the balloons very closely. He notes even the slightest resemblances to the stringed bumps on his head. As the balloons come closer he becomes more intent. He is enthralled with the potential of these concepts. He searches his mind for associated ideas. He reaches out, takes a firm grip on the strings, and begins to tie them securely to his previous knowledge. These new ideas are now his. This third attitude is a must for the listener.

THE HIGH ART OF CONCENTRATION

"Listen son of mine to what I say: Listen carefully" (4:20).

One of the popular stories of hospital life tells of two doctors meeting in the hospital corridor. The orthopedic surgeon is commiserating with the psychiatrist, "I don't know how you can spend all your day listening to people. . ."

The psychiatrist replies, "Who listens?"

Who indeed? Listening is really hard work. It calls for the expenditure of effort in concentrating to defeat our listening inertia. Listening cannot be carried on as a part-time activity; it must be entered into with all the vigor we can muster.

Returning from the rural area where I was pastoring my first church, I thrilled with excitement at the prospect of seeing my former pastor. I had so many stories to tell him. Entering his office, we shook hands and then sat down as I started to recount my story.

Bubbling over with enthusiasm, I poured out my tale. To my amazement my friend didn't even look me in the eyes. He straightened up his desk top, pushed sundry pens and pencils into place, leaned over to pull out a drawer, and moved around its contents. Now and then he half-glanced my way.

My story slowed down. Its importance gradually diminished, and finally I limped to a conclusion, made a lame excuse, and left his office. It was one of the most disappointing encounters of my life.

In a later, frank interview the man confessed he had really been interested in what I had to tell but merely wanted to make the most use of his time—hence his tidying-up effort. He might have finished with a neat desk, but he had ruined a relationship. He had not learned to listen.

During World War II, Australian women industriously knitted socks for soldiers. At any and every meeting they considered it their patriotic duty to keep knitting needles constantly on the move. They undoubtedly were the most difficult of all groups to which to speak. Clicking needles and vacant faces that told the story of mental calculations of stitches and patterns were absolutely no inspiration for a speaker.

And make no mistake about it: A listening audience

is more than half the secret of any successful speech. A group with any sizable number of people who refuse to take an interest in the speaker can transform an eloquent orator into a halting, hesitant, dry-as-dust talker.

Since writing the foregoing I stumbled on a passage from the writings of Charles Haddon Spurgeon. Sometimes called the "Prince of Preachers," Spurgeon was one of the adornments of the Victorian era. Five or six thousand people jammed his church morning and evening every Sunday for years. With no musical instruments or complex educational organization in his church, the sermon was the main feature of the service. This brilliant orator had a preaching ability rarely heard before or since.

Among other activities he organized a theological college for the training of ministers. His lectures to these students are gems of wit and wisdom. In one of the lectures on the subject of "attention" he voiced his reaction to inattentive auditors: ". . . they are not in the habit of attending. They attend the chapel but do not attend to the preacher. They are accustomed to look around at every one who enters the place, and they come in at all times, sometimes with much stamping, squeaking of boots, and banging of doors. I was preaching once to a people who continually looked around, and I adopted the wisdom of saying, 'Now friends, as it is so very interesting to you to know who comes in, and it disturbs me so very much for you to look around, I will, if you like, describe each one as he comes in, so that you may sit and look at me, and keep up at least a show of decency.' I described one gentleman who came in, who happened to be a friend whom I could depict without offense, as 'a very respectable gentleman who had just taken his hat off,' and so on; and after that one attempt I found it was not necessary to describe anymore, because they felt shocked at what I was doing, and I assured them that I was much more shocked that they should render it necessary for me to reduce their conduct to such absurdity. It cured them for the time being, and I hope forever, much to their pastor's joy." [1]

The distressed preacher went on to describe how people who were not listening affected him. He maintained that he wanted all eyes fixed on him and all ears opened to him. He added, "To me it is an annoyance if even a blind man does not look me in the face."

What was true of the preacher and his audience is equally true of the speaker and his listener. The way in which the listener pays attention to a conversational partner will in a large measure determine the quality of the conversation.

Although nonprofessionals refer to a deaf person's lipreading, some professionals are not enthusiastic about the use of this term. They point out that the so-called lip-reader doesn't just look at the lips but receives a number of visual cues. Some of them prefer the term "visual listening." The same principle applies to people who may have the acutest hearing: If you are to get the message, you must not listen with your ears alone but also visually read by concentrating on the speaker.

If you are going to be an effective listener, you must give the speaker your undivided attention. It is his moment, and every aspect of your demeanor must say, "Come on. Let's have it. You're in the center of the stage in my thinking."

The good listener doesn't do a lot of things. He cannot lean back in his chair with eyes half-closed as if he were taking his afternoon nap—none of those furtive looks as if mentally cataloging the books on his shelves. He doesn't steal glances at his watch with the inference, "Time is up; you've been here long enough." He won't doodle on a pad as though preparing an entry for a museum of modern art.

The good listener is relaxed. The telephone is cared for, his secretary warned against interruptions. He leans slightly toward the speaker, his eyes focused on him, not in a staring match, but in a coaxing, interested manner. Every aspect of the listening one says, "Tell me more."

Watch your speaker blossom as be becomes aware of the situation. See the way in which he drops his defenses; note the growing confidence in his bearing. Far too long he has been on the receiving end, and now he has a chance to express his ideas.

The good listener is a man with a mission. Every power of body and mind is focused on the listening task. As Solomon said it, "Listen carefully" (4:20).

THE REWARDS

"Hear, O my son, and receive my sayings; and the years of thy life shall be many" (4:10).
As we begin to listen we discover a whole new skill of living in relating to other people, but a far greater reward can be ours. When George Washington Carver, famous black scientist, appeared before a committee of the Congress, he was asked how he had made so many remarkable discoveries about horticulture. His response, "I get up early in the mornings and I go out into the woods and listen for the voice of God."

If we learn to listen all sorts of things will happen. We will become better husbands, wives, family members, employers, supervisors. But preeminently if we learn to *really* listen, it may be said of us—as it was of one in a bygone day—"And thine ears shall hear a word behind thee saying this is way, walk ye in it" (Isa. 30:21, KJV). If we hear this voice we are blessed indeed.

PROVERBS ON LISTENING

Proverbs 2:1   *Proverbs 5:7*
Proverbs 4:1   *Proverbs 7:24*
Proverbs 4:10   *Proverbs 8:3*
Proverbs 4:20   *Proverbs 8:4–5*
Proverbs 5:1   *Proverbs 8:6*

Proverbs 8:33

11

PROVERBIAL MONEY MANAGEMENT

Wisdom gives riches.   *Proverbs 3:16*

Does the book of Proverbs come from a simple period in history devoid of the complications which arise in a capitalistic era in which money and its evils have reared their ugly heads? Don't kid yourself.

This unusual volume discusses many subjects, but none more than money, what it represents, how it is gained, what it means, and what should be done with it. If you make an analysis of Proverbs you will discover there are something like forty-eight references to money, wealth, riches, and property. Apparently the financial problems faced by people in everyday twentieth-century life are by no means unique to this age. Proverbs may help us to see the relationship of money, family, and faith.

During the Reformation era some religious expressions took rather extreme forms. One early chronicler reports the case if a peasant, Hans Ber. This man felt a sudden call from God to go forth to preach. He arose in the middle of the night and announced to his wife that he must leave her and the children to follow the divine command.

His wife, naturally upset at this sudden development complained that by neglecting his family obligation he was denying his faith.

Let us apply this principle to our situation. Simply put, it means that one of the evidences of a virile faith is our concern for the well-being of our family and viable plan to care for their welfare. One of the best places for guidelines on this matter is the book of Proverbs which has so much sound counsel on the subject.

HOW IMPORTANT IS MONEY?

"Lazy men are soon poor; hard workers get rich" (10:4).
Many a thoughtful Christian has spent some time pondering the place of money in the believer's life. The Bible abounds with warnings about the dangers of money and Jesus warned his followers about a crass materialistic attitude towards life that caused people to overlook the place of spiritual values. He cautioned about the dangers of storing up treasures on earth rather than in heaven and made his unequivocal declaration, "It is almost impossible for a rich man to get into the Kingdom of heaven" (Matt. 19:23). However, we should note it is not money itself but what we do with money. Money representing honest labor has a strange connection with Christianity.

One of the significant and unintended byproducts of the Reformation movement was to place new value on honest toil. Before Martin Luther's day the idea of "vocation" or "calling" was that special people were called of God to the special task of entering a monastery where they studied the "counsels of perfection." Ordinary Christians followed the commandments of God. Luther rejected this idea. He said, "There is no special religious vocation since the call of God comes to each man at the common tasks."

The expression, "vocational guidance," by which we mean helping people to prepare themselves for a life's work, stems from Luther. Luther said God himself works at a common vocation, creating and sustaining the world. When we work with our hands we are helping God who has no hands but our hands, no feet but our feet. Luther defended lowly tasks, "The lowlier the task the better. The milkmaid and the carter of manure are doing work more pleasing to God than the psalm singing of the Carthusian."

According to Max Weber who wrote *The Protestant Ethic and the Spirit of Capitalism,* this attitude was in large measure responsible for the rise of capitalism. The Reformation attitude was that work was God's calling, and so man worked hard. Each revival of religion helped to reinforce the idea that, rather than being a penalty for sin, as the Catholic church maintained, work was an activity of worth in its own right. A second element was the puritanical conviction that personal indulgence should be avoided. Each wave of revival brought new motivations to practice self-denial. As Wesley stated it, "Religion must necessarily produce industry and frugality." So hard work + frugality = accumulation. The natural result of these two factors was the accumulation of wealth—thus the spirit of capitalism was the unintended byproduct of the Reformation.

It could be argued that the wealth and prosperity of the United States have been in some measure due to the influence of the Protestant ethic. Significantly the U.S. has in turn produced many vigorous churches which, because of their influence, have been able to play a large part in disseminating the gospel message across the world. Money, rightly used, can play an important part in the ongoing work of the kingdom of Christ.

PRINCIPLES OF MONEY MANAGEMENT

"Don't withhold payment of your debts. Don't say 'some other time' if you can pay now" (3:27–28).

"Son, if you endorse a note for someone you hardly

know, guaranteeing his debt, you are in serious trouble"
(6:1).

Even in Solomon's day people had difficulties in managing
their money, and Proverbs has many warnings about the
necessity for being wise in money management, paying off
debts, lending money, and the like. What would Solomon
say today if he saw the multiplicity of pressures brought to
bear on people in the hope of persuading them to part with
their hard-earned cash? We might need to remind ourselves
that as difficult as it can be to earn money that difficulty
fades into insignificance when we face the problem of what
to do with it. Strictly speaking spending is not difficult at
all. It is all too easy and therein lies the heart of the problem. Money is much easier to spend than it is to earn.

At first glance deciding how the family money is to
be dispersed seems fairly simple. Certain obligations must
be met, and you sit down and weigh the pros and cons, consider the alternatives, and go ahead and spend it. But alas
the disbursal of money from the family treasury is seldom
just a logical procedure.

In terms of the number of people affected by his
teaching, there probably never was a more influential
theorist about money than Karl Marx. His economic theo-
ries have rocked the world, but how did he do with his own
finances? A sympathetic biographer wrote about Marx.
"Regular work bored him, conventional occupation put him
out of humor. Without a penny in his pocket and with his
shirt pawned, he surveyed the world with a lordly air and
detested social intercourse on equal terms. He only cared to
clink glasses with persons who praised and admired him.
Throughout his life he was hard up. He was ridiculously
ineffectual in his endeavors to cope with the economic needs
of his household and his family. And his incapacity in
monetary matters involved him in an endless series of
struggles and catastrophes. He was always in debt. He was

incessantly being dunned by creditors, persecuted by usurers, half his household goods were always in the pawn shop. His budget defied all attempts to set it in order. His bankruptcy was chronic. The thousands upon thousands which his friend Engles handed over to him melted away in his fingers like snow." [1]

If Karl Marx, the economic theorist who was an expert on national finances, couldn't manage his money, what chance do you and I have? The main lesson of Marx is that money management is much more emotional than intellectual, and people handle finances in a manner that is going to satisfy their emotional needs. Psychologists have long noted this emotional factor in handling finances, and marriage counselors are vividly aware of the relationship of emotions and spending practices.

John and Susie Harris are having a difficult experience. John is the "big spender" when out with the boys or entertaining company, with the result that Susie has trouble balancing the domestic budget. She demands, "Why go 'round picking up tabs and buying drinks when you can't pick up the tab on the expenses of your own home and family?"

William and Carmen Scott had it all carefully planned before their marriage. Carmen would continue working, but they would live on William's salary and use Carmen's to build a savings account. Carmen periodically goes on a spending spree. When William questions the new mink coat she says, "It's my money; I earned it."

Harry and Jean Smith can *just* manage on their income. Harry hasn't done well in his job. But on anniversaries or Jean's birthday he buys the most lavish gifts. Jean accepts them with despair rather than gratitude. She knows they can't afford them.

Tom and Verna Barker agreed that Verna would not work outside the home. Tom prided himself on his business acumen, so he took over management of the family finances. He developed an aggravating way of doling out the money. Verna found herself constantly in the position of explaining why she had made certain expenditures and having to almost plead for extra money.

In each of these cases money was being used for other than financial purposes. John Harris, the big spender, is building up his ego at the expense of his family. Carmen Scott by having "her money" is maintaining her independence from her husband. Harry Smith giving his wife extravagant gifts is trying to buy her love and respect. Tom Barker is using money as a way of dominating his wife.

A study in one counseling center showed that almost half the people who came for marital counseling reported money problems. Yet closer examination revealed that only a small proportion of these—about 6 percent were in difficulty because of inadequate income or financial stringency. Obviously, then, money is one of the emotional battlegrounds within a marriage relationship.

But isn't more money the *real answer* to financial problems? Let's be realistic. Throughout life you are probably not going to have as much money as you would like, and you will lament your lack of finances.

Once again you have company. One study showed that at each income level most Americans wanted just 25 percent more, but the moment they got such a raise new needs began to emerge, and they were soon in trouble again. The rule seems to be that expenses always rise to meet increases in incomes. The main problem is not the *amount earned* but rather the *way we manage it,* and this is where those troublesome emotions get in our way.

The situation has been aptly summarized: "We have *unlimited dreams* but *limited funds.*" In our unlimited dreams we may see ourselves owning a new *color TV,* an *elaborate wardrobe,* a *sports car,* a *home of our own,* a *cot-*

tage at the lake, a *yacht,* or taking leisurely trips around the world. As we finger a catalog, wander through a store, or view a new house or automobile, our imagination easily takes off, and we forget the commandment which warns us not to covet.

But let's face it—we have *limited funds.* The money left over after withholding taxes, etc., and all our regular commitments have been met is sometimes called our *discretionary* income. How discreet can we be with it?

Amid all the advertising pressures on every hand, we will always be tempted to overspend. It is easy to fall into one of three categories of spenders.

Competitive spenders. Competition is the essence of our way of life. As manufacturers compete against each other they improve the quality of their goods and services. So competition is good.

But competition is bad. Bad when you compete with other people trying to keep up with the Joneses. In this frame of mind you buy items you don't really need, and they become status symbols. Symbols that may in turn become monuments to a financially bankrupt family.

Compulsive spenders. It seems strange, but there are some people who actually *feel* better when they are spending money. Women will often say, "I was feeling down in the dumps, so I just went out on a spending spree and that made me feel better."

The main difficulty is that a money problem might have been a factor in her depression. Now by going on a spending spree, while she gained a temporary exhilaration, she must now face a more complicated financial problem. People in this category are like alcoholics, only their problems come from money rather than the bottle. They have what some psychologists call a compulsion. Even though they know that it is futile to continue spending money, they continue on their self-defeating way.

Significantly the word guilt comes from an Anglo-Saxon word which means "to pay." In Yiddish, the word *gelt* means money. Of guilt Paul Tournier says, "It is inscribed on the human heart, everything must be paid for." And McKenzie asserts, "Guilt must be paid for."

One personality theorist speaks about *Psychoeconomics,* a term which describes the need to make some type of payment, and the psychic or even physical pain may be a means of doing just that.

It may take an even more direct form. One woman came to a counseling center to tell her story. Although in a high-income bracket, she nevertheless continued to spend more than her husband earned. She embarked on wild shopping sprees and had closets full of clothes she had never worn, yet would go out and buy more. As she progressed in counseling she was able to face up to some areas of failure in her life as a wife and a mother. As she acknowledged these failures she was able to get her spending habits under control.

If you are a big spender you might profit from an experience of self-examination in which you are willing to face some hidden area of irresponsibility in your life, acknowledge it, and take some positive action, rather than continue to pay in such a self-defeating way.

Impulsive spenders. One man said his wife was like Teddy Roosevelt. She rushed into the stores shouting, "Charge!" You will always be tempted by the sign of some attractive and apparently valuable item and want it. All of us are given to acting on impulse. One woman said her favorite recipe was

> 2 well-scrubbed kids
> 1 buttered-up Daddy
> 1 fist full of dough
> Place in a well-greased car and
> head for the restaurant.

Remember that when you go shopping, you are always tempted to buy on the impulse. Here are a few ideas that might help you.

(1) Set a shopping budget, and stick to it.

(2) Always make a list before you go shopping.

(3) Be bargain-conscious, but not at the expense of buying things you never use.

(4) Don't be afraid to put things back after you have taken them off the shelf, or to return them after you have brought them home. The after-thoughts may be more worthwhile than the impulse.

(5) Shop around and read the ads, but don't be bowled over by carefully devised sales lures.

(6) Get what you really need, not what you think you might use someday.

(7) Before you make a major purchase, think it over carefully. Try to hold off for a day or two.

(8) Leave the children at home when you shop. Advertisers say that they are great expediters of shopping impulses, especially in the TV age.

Learn the principles of money management and you will have the battle of family finances, if not won, at least well under control.

A FAMILY SAVINGS PLAN

". . . give me neither poverty nor riches. Give me just enough to satisfy my needs" (30:8).

If we are going to have enough money to satisfy our needs, we must have some good plan of saving, particularly with inflation gnawing away at the value of our precious dollars. A good principle is——PAY YOURSELF FIRST.

If a close relative of yours died and left you $202,800 (after taxes) you'd probably spend a good deal of attention to the care and management of the inheritance, wouldn't you? Well, $202,800 is what you can expect if you average a mere $70 a week (take-home pay) for the first twenty years of your life and $100 a week (take-home pay) for the last twenty-five years until retirement at age sixty-five. Why not give this $200,000 plus the attention it deserves, and quit spreading it over the economy without keeping a few cents for yourself. Remember, a part of all you earn is yours to keep.

One widely used definition of maturity is, *"Maturity is the capacity to postpone pleasure."* One counseling center reported that more and more people are overspending the family budgets for what they call *instant gratification.* They must have all their desires satisfied *at once.*

I once attended a meeting of pre-release convicts. The men were asked to stand before the group and tell how they landed in trouble. Over and over again I heard their statements, "I couldn't wait." "I wanted a car so I stole it." "I wanted sex so I raped." Instant gratification but also misery and despair!

The Bible is filled with instances of the principle that maturity is the capacity to postpone pleasure. In the Old Testament story of Joseph he gained favor by interpreting Pharaoh's dream and prophesying there would be seven years of plenty followed by seven years of famine.

When Pharaoh appointed Joseph to prepare a plan for the lean years, the astute young Hebrew produced one that was the essence of simplicity. During the seven bountiful years he carefully bought great supplies of corn and stored it away. When the lean and barren years followed, Joseph had the food available to see the Egyptian people over the starvation years.

The unexpected family benefit came when Joseph's family, not knowing who he was, came searching for food. Joseph was able to provide them with ample food and a place to live.

Jesus asked his followers just how they would go about building a tower. He said that the first and obvious step was for a man to count his money and find out if he had enough money to complete it. The danger, he said, was that people might laugh and say, "He began to build, but he couldn't complete it."

You need to look to the future and save your money. Here are seven reasons why you should save.

1. As a "financial cushion" for emergencies such as serious illness, accident or unemployment.
2. For large recurring expenses such as insurance premiums and real estate taxes.
3. For large non-recurring expenses such as furniture, home improvement and decorating bills or an expensive item of clothing such as a fur coat.
4. For short term goals such as a vacation, Christmas and birthday gifts, a car, TV set or appliances.
5. For long term goals such as wedding, travel, down payment towards the purchase of a home or college education for your children.
6. To take advantage of opportunities for personal advancement, business success or investment profit.
7. To supplement Social Security, a company retirement plan, insurance annuity, unemployment or disability insurance, group hospitalization and medical benefits.

How much of your income should you save?

Some experts say 5 to 10 percent of your take-home pay; others would increase this to 10 to 20 percent. If you sit down and figure what saving can do for you, you may be surprised.

Supposing you decided to save just $5 per week at the low rate of 5 percent on savings. Do you realize that if you did this for a twenty-year period you would finish up with $8,940.16. You would have invested $5,200, and you would have received a whopping $2,740.16 in interest.

Remember—*A part of all you earn is yours to keep.* And if you keep it in the right place it will keep right on earning.

Two considerations vital to a good savings plan:

(1) *Save first.* Many people wait to see what they have left over. This doesn't generally amount to much. Put away your savings first of all; then proceed with the rest of your program.

(2) *Save regularly.* If you can, get into some withholding plan or buy savings bonds. Anything that will compel you to save a portion of each pay check.

John Wesley, founder of Methodism, gave his followers some good counsel which is applicable to our situation today. It was, "Save all you can."

USING YOUR FAMILY IN MONEY MANAGEMENT

"She watches for bargains" (31:18).

"A father can give his sons homes and riches" (19:14).

The practicalities of family finances are such that the secret of it all lies in a plan of practical money management. You must start, whether you like it or not, with a budget. It's going to take time, patience, and emotional maturity for you to develop an adequate budget.

You must be realistic about the whole process, especially your income, which you will be tempted to overestimate. You have probably heard the story of the holdup man. He suddenly appeared at the paymaster's window of a large plant and demanded, "Never mind the payroll, bud, just hand me the welfare funds, the group insurance premiums, the pension fund, the union dues, the medical de-

ductions, and the withholding taxes." This story serves to
show the difference between your gross incomes and your
take-home pay. Assess it realistically.

Once you've decided to set up your budget, you will
need to project some realistic administrative plan. In some
homes the husband insists on handling the money and feels
threatened if his wife attempts to interfere in the family
finances. However, just being a man doesn't mean that you
automatically have financial acumen.

Martin Luther stood every inch a man, but he always had trouble managing his money. When he married
Katherine Von Bora he was already forty-two years old and
penniless. He took no profits from the sale of his books and
had never bothered to save money. Although he was a remarkable man in many ways he was a money management
dropout. Whatever money he received slipped through his
fingers. In a mastery of understatement he said on one occasion, "I do not believe I can be accused of niggardliness."
He openly stated a policy which would have irked a modern
domestic finance expert, "I do not worry about debts because when Katie pays for one, another one comes."

So Katie took charge. Their banker learned never
to honor a draft unless Katherine first approved of it. She
strictly limited her husband, as is seen in a letter he wrote:
"I am sending you a vase for a wedding present. P.S. Katie
hid it."

The man who rocked the Holy Roman Empire and
withstood the might of the Pope and emperor was himself,
in the financial affairs of life, under the strict control of his
ex-nun wife.

But does it have to be an either/or proposition?

Why not involve the whole family in this process of
handling the money? It has a number of features to commend it.

(1) Many problems are avoided when family mem-

bers realize no one is making a decision just for himself but one which will affect all the members of the family.

(2) If you run into a financial crisis and it's necessary to curtail spending, it's much easier if all the family members know why the crises has arisen and share in reaching the decision.

(3) Because all the family will know what is happening, there is less likelihood of personal conflicts about money matters.

Following this scheme the husband and wife form economic partnership with the children participating as junior partners. The family members can then learn to play certain roles that parallel those of a business concern. Here are the roles suggested by the American Home Economics Association family finances specialists:

(1) The *board of directors* sets policy and plays the key role. In the family, husband and wife play this role jointly, and the board may also include children.

(2) The *general manager* is the "watchdog," responsible for seeing that board policy is carried out by all members and generally making sure that everything runs smoothly.

(3) *The paymaster* pays the bills. He writes the checks and oversees the daily flow of cash.

(4) The *purchasing agent* does the buying. All family members play this role on occasion, depending on the kind of purchasing being done.

(5) The *bookkeeper* keeps the financial records, balancing the budget and the checkbook.

(6) The *apprentice* is normally the child's role, but there are times when one of the adult partners may also need financial training.

(7) The *training officer* instructs the apprentice in money management and supervises his economic education.

Because women do most of the spending in the

US wives are bound to play a larger purchasing-agent role. Because men are often the breadwinners and carry the authority of family heads, husbands often fill the role of general manager. But there's no "right" or typical way to assign the husband's and wife's financial duties.

Each family should find its own style. This will mean discovering who has particular aptitude for what. The purchasing agent must know the available products and their prices, and the family bookkeeper will generally be the person with a knack for figures.

The need to make decisions on who plays what role provides the perfect occasion for a board of directors meeting. Many families have board meetings without planning them. They "meet" spontaneously at dinner, when working in the yard, or on similar occasions. Others meet only in emergencies, such as when a major appliance needs replacing, or in special situations, say, when a job change comes up or at income tax time.

Planned, periodic meetings are probably desirable, perhaps scheduled for a specific time at least once each month. A good time may be when you receive the monthly bank statement, which in itself mirrors your past spending and can reflect progress toward goals.

Once the board is operating, it considers the total income of the family and makes decisions on short- and long-term spending, investments, insurance, savings, borrowing, and retirement funds. Its meeting is also the place for special requests and even complaints—but not for anger or tears. Nor should the board waste time on trivial decisions, such as what brand of soap to buy. That's best left to the purchasing agent. But a "major-purchase" decision to buy a new car, to invest in stock, or perhaps even to buy a new suit may require family discussion. What constitutes a "major purchase," of course, depends on the family's resources.

In the long run, the policy decisions are much more

important than who carries them out in what role. If the
directors make sound decisions, the family enterprise will
succeed.

THE PRINCIPLE OF TRUE WEALTH

"It is possible to give away and become richer! It is
also possible to hold on too tightly and lose everything.
Yes, the liberal man shall be rich! By watering others, he
waters himself" (11:24–25).
The writer of this immensely practical book is realistic in
his evaluation of the effects of money on people. Counting
up the proverbs dealing with the subject of money, it will
be seen that some thirty-six times they warn of the dangers
that may come from the misuse of money.

The overall thrust of the biblical message is that
everything belongs to God—consequently a man is only a
steward of his possessions. In Australia the capital is a
magnificent city called Canberra. It is one of the few capital
cities in the world which was planned and designed, then
built on a piece of open countryside. The city has been kept
in much of this atmosphere, and it is a beautiful spot. Parliament House where the legislators gather looks across a
great basin to one of the most impressive war memorials in
the world. The theory is that the legislators coming and
going from Parliament House will be reminded of the cost
of wars and the importance of the decisions they make.

Probably the most interesting single feature of Canberra is that all the land is owned by the federal government. All users of land must lease it; no one can ever own
that land. It belongs to the government. Similarly, the Bible
teaches us that God is the Creator, and he owns everything.
Whatever possessions we might have at any given moment
are simply the things that are owned by God. We are his
stewards, and we are responsible for handling these possessions in a way that will bring honor and glory to his name.

Using an appropriate metaphor, the Bible asks the

hypothetical question, "Will a man rob God?" The dialog follows:

> GOD: "Ye have robbed me!"
> PEOPLE: "Wherein have we robbed thee?"
> GOD: "In tithes and offerings."

The tithe, a tenth of one's income, would seem the minimum contribution we could make with the possibilities that offerings might be made in addition.

Another theme is giving. Paul reminded his readers Jesus' statement unrecorded in the Gospels, "Ye remember the words of our Lord Jesus, It is more blessed to give than to receive." John Bunyan had the same idea:

> *There was a man,*
> *Folks thought him mad,*
> *The more he gave,*
> *The more he had.*

John Wesley, having urged his people to earn all they could and save as much as possible, considered the possible effects of so much money and added a third rule:

> *Earn all you can,*
> *Save all you can,*
> *Give all you can.*

What is true wealth? There are many things that are more valuable than money.

Righteousness: "Your riches won't help you on Judgment Day; only righteousness counts then" (11:4).

A Good Name: "If you must choose, take a good name rather than great riches" (22:1).

Humility: "Better poor and humble than proud and rich" (16:19).

Honesty: "Better be poor and honest than rich and dishonest" (19:1).

Peace of mind: "Some rich people are poor, and some poor people have great wealth! Being kidnapped and held for ransom never worries the poor man!" (13:7–8).

PROVERBIAL TEACHINGS
ABOUT MONEY

Proverbs 2:3–5	*Proverbs 16:19*
Proverbs 3:13–15	*Proverbs 18:11*
Proverbs 3:16–17	*Proverbs 18:23*
Proverbs 5:10	*Proverbs 19:1*
Proverbs 7:20	*Proverbs 19:14*
Proverbs 8:18	*Proverbs 21:17*
Proverbs 10:3	*Proverbs 22:1*
Proverbs 10:4	*Proverbs 22:2*
Proverbs 10:15	*Proverbs 22:4*
Proverbs 10:22	*Proverbs 22:7*
Proverbs 11:4	*Proverbs 23:1*
Proverbs 11:16	*Proverbs 23:4–5*
Proverbs 11:18	*Proverbs 24:19–20*
Proverbs 11:28	*Proverbs 24:23*
Proverbs 11:24–25	*Proverbs 27:23–24*
Proverbs 13:7	*Proverbs 28:6*
Proverbs 13:11	*Proverbs 28:11*
Proverbs 13:22	*Proverbs 28:20*
Proverbs 13:23	*Proverbs 28:21*
Proverbs 14:20	*Proverbs 28:22*
Proverbs 15:27	*Proverbs 29:13*
Proverbs 16:8	*Proverbs 30:8*

Proverbs 30:9

12

PROVERBIAL DISCIPLINE

If you refuse to discipline your son it proves you
don't love him; for if you love him you will be prompt to
punish him.   *Proverb 13:24*

The small boy was protesting loudly because his mother had carefully explained the reasons why she couldn't allow him to go, all to no avail. He stamped his feet, cried, and yelled. Feeling she was reaching breaking point the mother finally said, "All right, then do what you want to." The distraught child was still not satisfied and responded, "I don't want to do what I want to do."

Poor parent, she was facing one of the problems of life in America today as we have entered into a period sometimes described as "child rule." Such an attitude cannot be justified in the family which is portrayed in the book of Proverbs. Probably the most widely known statement on discipline is the maxim, "Spare the rod and spoil the child," but a close examination of Proverbs shows this is not what it says. The King James Version has it, "He that spareth his rod, hateth his child" (13:24, KJV). Notice the difference. It isn't a matter of the effect on the child but rather a revelation of the concern of the parent. So, in *The Living Bible* the statement is translated, "If you refuse to discipline your son, it proves you don't love him, for if you love him you will be prompt to punish him" (13:24). Love and discipline go hand in hand and only the parent who pays close attention to the family takes time to teach them the lessons they need to learn.

Much has been written in recent days about people who talk with plants. Practitioners of these skills tell about how they communicate with their favorite plants and the manner in which these plants respond with improved growth, flowers, or fruit. A recent article about growing African violets gave a list of instructions about how to cultivate these plants, and the final piece of instruction on the list was, "Love them." Love them??

Talking the matter over with a psychologist friend, I referred to the article and laughed skeptically, "Whatever on earth is all this nonsense about loving an African violet?"

I knew this hard-headed scientific researcher would come up with some witty, cynical response. But alas for my hopes. Unbeknown to me he, too, had fallen under the influence of the indoor houseplant craze, and he answered, "Have you ever thought that love means to pay attention, water and fertilize them, keep a close eye on them?"

Of course he was correct, and he had unwittingly ushered me into the first great principle of the establishment of behavior.

THE GREATEST REWARD I CAN GIVE IS ATTENTION!

THE POWER OF ATTENTION

We may have missed the most important aspects of behavior as it is described in the book of Proverbs. We have been hard at work thinking about the rod when we should have noted the other factors that change behavior, particularly for the better. In contrast to many of the women mentioned in Proverbs who scold, nag, are quarrelsome, or of easy virtue, there is an amazing woman in the concluding chapter who has apparently become the model for Jewish women across the ages. The secret of her behavior is seen in how she was given attention:

> *Her children stand up and bless her, so does her husband. He praises her with these words, "There are many wonderful women in the world but you are the best of them all." Charm can be deceptive and beauty doesn't last, but a woman who fears and reverences God shall be greatly praised. Praise her for all the many fine things she does. These good deeds of hers shall bring her honor and recognition from even the leaders of the nations (Praise her in the gates) (31:28–31).*

As compared to the few words about "the rod," in this single passage "praise" or a synonym is used five times in the description of this woman, and therein lies the secret of her remarkable performance.

Attention is the greatest reward one individual can give another. The manager of a hamburger enterprise understood this principle. This enterprise was booming, and I could not understand why. This particular business had limped along for a number of years, and now it had new management, and customers were crowding in to buy their hamburgers and other goodies.

Being something of a connoisseur of this noble product of the American culinary skill, I joined the throng and invested in a "Super Deluxe Burger," which cost twice as much as I normally shelled out for.

The burger was—well—okay. So I was delighted a few weeks later when I sat alongside the manager at a civic club meeting.

I asked him, "What is it that you have that other hamburger businesses lack? There are hamburger joints all over this town, and none of them are doing the sort of business you are. To be really frank, I'm not sure the 'Super

Burger' is any better than the 'Giant Gastro' or the 'Monster Master.' "

The manager smiled, "We use about the same meat, perhaps a little better quality, lettuce and tomato, but in addition to these we add one other important ingredient—service."

Then I recollected those smartly dressed kids who manned his business. One cute girl welcomed the patron at the door, another at the counter pleasantly greeted the client, "Can I help you?" I was the center of attention.

The manager went on to explain that his most difficult task was to train his staff to make the customer the center of their attention. Employees were carefully instructed to always smile, warmly welcome the customer—no standing around talking to each other—in other words, make the customer king.

I have become an addicted fan of that place. I go there for the same reason as do most other customers—I like the service—the attention those employees give.

What do people want most of all in life? Beautiful home? Lake house? High salary? Security? The latest model automobile? Trip around the world? No, none of these. People want ATTENTION.

People need attention, and much of their behavior is carried on in terms of the attention they get. But attention itself comes in a variety of forms. The highest form of attention is praise. Any behavior which is praised will probably be maintained so the idea is simple: if you see some behavior you like, then praise it.

Look for something to praise rather than criticize. Our little dog had grown old but not very gracefully. At one stage in his career, he had been involved in a fight from which he emerged with one eye badly damaged. As a result, this eye had a bad habit of turning in the wrong direction and showing a white area that gave him a somewhat sinister appearance.

The passing years had also brought on an arthritic condition that settled in his left rear leg. As it became more painful, the little dog gave up using the sore limb and made a rather pathetic picture as he limped along on three legs.

Because he found handling so painful, we had given up on having him clipped and also combing his hair. A French poodle with long, unkempt hair does not present a very attractive sight.

Ginger Hazelton, eleven years old, was visiting our home. On her best behavior, she was commending everything in our house, and when she faced the poodle, her capacity to commend met its supreme test.

There stood that poodle, one leg painfully drawn up under him, an eye that made him look like a canine Peter Lorre, his uneven matted hair giving him the appearance of a dried-out mop. Ginger's attention to detail provided her with a response, giving her the opening she needed as she commented, "He certainly knows how to wag his tail."

If you look long enough you will find something to commend. In this way you will help your subject do something about developing his potential.

Make your praise descriptive. Some enthusiast reading about the use of praise is likely to say, "Well, if running around flattering people is all I have to do, I can easily manage that." So he starts pouring out syrupy compliments commending mediocrity and winning his way by flattery. While this line of attack may go over with some people for a short time, there's a good chance that in the long run a big proportion of people see through him, and he will antagonize many of his subjects.

Practitioners of these techniques of saccharine and syrup overlook the all-important factor of satiation. I am very fond of a little of that gastronomic delight called chili, but one cold day, in a fit of enthusiasm, I ordered a large bowl. By the time I had finished I suffered a loss of interest in that dish. My appetite was quickly satiated. With the satiation factor in mind, we will not praise indiscriminately, but when we do praise, we will make the praise descriptive.

Dr. Ronald Smith is a remarkably successful neurosurgeon with a talented and vivacious wife and the father of a bevy of beautiful girls.

This unusual medico is enormously popular with the staffs of the hospitals where he works, and many of his patients almost worship him. When his name is mentioned during the bridge game, the women "oohh" and "aahh," murmuring, "He's darling." Many of them go on to recall stories of friends, acquaintances, and relatives who have been saved from death by this doctor's diagnostic and surgical skills.

Dr. Smith is a man of parts. The lovely trophy room in his beautiful house, adorned with the heads of wild beasts, leopard, zebra, impala, Gran's gazelle, onyx, topi, kudu, water buck, and elephant tusks bears mute evidence of his prowess as a big-game hunter. His greenhouse over from the swimming pool, in his carefully manicured yard, contains exotic flowers that bear evidence of his horticultural interest, and his collection of antique jade indicates his capacity as a collector of beautiful things. And there is no doubting the abilities he demonstrates as he performs delicate surgery on the human brain and nervous system.

However, this remarkable man has yet another skill unrelated to surgical capacity, but in many ways the key to his tremendous popularity. He has an unusual capacity to commend people. He adopts a unique way of doing this.

When examining the X-rays, he turns to the technician and says, "These certainly are wonderful X-rays. You really know how to get the exact position that I need." Looking at the patient swathed in bandages he tells the nurse, "If an ancient Egyptian Pharaoh had ever heard

about you, he would certainly have employed you as ban-
dager of the royal mummies." Sitting for long hours watching his neighbor's slides and the interminable commentary,
he remarks, "That picture from the Star Ferry in Hong
Kong shows the way a good shot can be framed and made
very attractive."

One friend of Dr. Smith's remarked, "Ronald would
have a good word to say about the devil!"

Learn from Dr. Smith. Particularize your praise.

Don't just say, "You're a good boy," but, "You did
a wonderful job on that lawn." Not, "You certainly help

Good	*Thank you.*
That's right.	*I'm pleased with that.*
That's clever.	
Excellent	*Great*
Exactly	*I like that.*
Good job	*I love you.*
Good thinking	*That's interesting.*
That shows a great deal of work.	*That's smart.*
You really pay attention.	*That was very kind of you.*
You should show this to your father.	
Show Grandma your picture.	

(Said to Father at dinner) Jimmy got right down to work after school, and his homework is done already.

our organization," but, "The way you handled that client was magnificent." Once again there is no shortcut; you must examine behavior.

Have some praise statements in mind. Unless you have a very good vocabulary, there is a chance that you won't find it easy to come up with the right word at the right time. Remembering how important it is to make praise descriptive; much will depend on the subject and the type of behavior you wish to strengthen.

In the preceding box are some of the statements that would be appropriate for use with children in strengthening their behavior.

Look over the situation you are working in. Examine the person you are trying to influence. Check him out. Find out some things about him that you can commend at the appropriate time. Prepare some statements and have them ready to use at the best time.

THE WAY TO PUNISH

Now we have established the principle that the greatest reward is to pay attention, it will lead us to a correlation. *The greatest punishment is withholding attention.*

Most visitors see the English city of Coventry as a great industrial center and the location of a majestic, modernistic cathedral built as a memorial to British servicemen who lost their lives in World War II.

Its claim to literary fame, though, is enshrined in the saying, "Send him to Coventry." The saying came originally from the king's unpopular practice of billeting his soldiers in private homes. The citizens of Coventry had such dislike for the imposition of troops on them that they refused to have anything to do with these soldiers. Any woman seen fraternizing with a soldier was immediately ostracized by her fellow citizens.

Because of this attitude, if a soldier were stationed

in Coventry, the attitude of the citizenry meant that he was cut off from all social contact. Consequently, men in the army dreaded an assignment to that city.

If you consult a dictionary of sayings you will find:

Send him to Coventry—*To take no notice, to isolate, or have no dealings with.*

It becomes obvious that the modern practitioners of this torture are far more subtle in their methods, so subtle that they would probably be astounded when told they had cultivated the cruel art of tormenting their fellows.

News of battered children has astonished America. One reliable source has estimated that in any one year there are thousands of battered children in the U.S. Despite all this physical punishment, battered children are perhaps not the worst victims of torture; the most exquisite suffering is experienced by children who are neglected, never commended or praised.

Orphanages and other institutions for children have provided dramatic evidence of what lack of attention does to these kids. In one period of time studied some years ago, almost all the children admitted to institutions under the age of one year failed to survive the first year of life.

One observer of this situation concluded that all the children needed was love. In an orphanage, a visitor noticed a large, motherly woman walking around with a child on her hip. When asked who she was the guide replied, "That's Emily. Whenever a child seems weak and sickly, we pass it over to Emily who takes it with her everywhere she goes. There is generally a dramatic improvement in the child's condition."

The famous psychiatrist, Smiley Blanton, has defined love as "An intense positive interest in an object." The interest is the great reward—deprivation of interest is the more intense punishment.

Once again Proverbs has a word for us, "Open rebuke is better than secret love" (27:6). Love that is unexpressed is of no avail.

Jason provides us with a good example of the way we may apply these principles. Jason's mother, Mrs. Crossly, works in a hospital on the night shift. A women of deep spiritual conviction, she wants her four children in Sunday School on Sunday morning. She hurries home from work, lays out their clothes, and proceeds to get them fed and ready for church. As they prepare to leave the house Jason emerges from his room wearing the weirdest array of clothes. Mrs. Crossly yells, "Jason, you've done it again. Come back in here. You naughty boy . . ."

As Mrs. Crossly told her story she said, "That's the way it is. I'm always yelling at him. He's always in trouble."

What do you say when Jason is good? "I don't say anything. I'm so mad with him for what he did wrong. I can't bring myself to commend him."

What was Mrs. Crossly doing? She was paying attention to bad behavior and ignoring good behavior. She was reversing the process. The best way is to praise good behavior and ignore bad behavior.

There are some principles involved in effective discipline.

1) *Stay calm and objective while disciplining.*

One woman advised not to punish her children when she was annoyed and upset responded, "Paddle him when I'm calm? If I'm not mad I can't bring myself to lay a hand on him."

Start by asking yourself why you are disciplining your child. If it is just to work off your own frustrations, you are failing miserably. By punishing the child when you are mad, you set the wrong model before him and may teach him the wrong lesson.

Remember the word "discipline" means "to teach."

Make the disciplining a real teaching experience by staying calm and dispassionate in the whole process—keep your cool.

2) *Timing is as important as discipline.*

Susannah Wesley, the mother of John Wesley, the founder of Methodism, lived in Epworth, England, in the early eighteenth century. A no-nonsense mother, she was the past master of the use of aversive conditioning. She believed in the biblical adage that if you spare the rod you spoil the child, and many of her methods, such as "breaking the child's spirit," would repel the modern child psychologist.

Nevertheless, in her disciplining procedures, Susannah Wesley showed an unusual awareness of the timing principle and how it should be used in aversive conditioning.

Most parents have faced the dilemma of children who get into some type of trouble, and when asked, "Why didn't you come and tell us about it?" the child answers, "I was frightened that if I told you, you would punish me."

In the use of aversive conditioning, the parent has actually trained the child to be dishonest and just not tell the truth.

Susannah overcame this problem with her sense of timing. As part of her set of rules, she had one which read, "Whenever a child did wrong and came and immediately confessed it, I did not punish that child."

This perceptive woman realized that if punishment came when the child was being honest, it would discourage honesty in the future. Timing is of the utmost significance in discipline.

In many families a problem with the children may reach a situation in which Mother gets mad and yells at Johnnie Lou, "Wait until Daddy comes home tonight—you'll get the paddling of your life."

Several possibilities present themselves. Johnnie

Lou may use her feminine wiles. She may call Daddy secretly on the phone and discuss a math problem which he can readily solve and volunteer to assist at the pancake supper his civic club is organizing later in the week. She may conclude the conversation by telling him that all the other kids say she has the best daddy on the block.

If Johnnie Lou is less sophisticated but goes all out to give him a warm welcome home, and Daddy follows through on the Mother's request, the event is so removed in time from the discipline that she may associate it with the experience which immediately preceded it, and decide there's not much sense in being nice to Daddy.

3) *Remember the pairing principle and couple warning signals with punishment.*

Mrs. Burdick has some problems with her overactive son Rick. He is always on the move, and this activity is seldom more irritating than when they are traveling in the car. As they move down the highway Rick waits until his mother is looking the other way, quickly releases his seat belt, and surreptitiously fastens it behind him. He is soon on his feet and standing up on the seat of the car.

Rick's mother sits down and explains, "The moment I spot you with your seat belt unfastened I will say, 'Check.' If you don't get it fastened within three seconds I will swat you. Got it?"

A phrase like, "Stop it," should be enunciated with the implication that unless there's action the ax will fall. If this pairing is observed, the warning words alone should be enough to get the job done in later experiences.

4) *Consistency is the keynote to effective discipline.*

Because we often want a quiet, uninterrupted life and feel we shouldn't always be on the children's backs, we generally don't discipline consistently but build up until we reach a point where we can't stand it any longer and then let fly.

When we recall the way behaviors are reinforced, we realize that every transgression must be acted upon. We should act every time. Conversely, the principle of intermittent reinforcement teaches us that if the child "gets away with it" every now and then the undesirable behavior is sustained.

Be consistent is the keynote of effective discipline.

THE MORE HE DISCIPLINED, THE GREATER PUNISHMENT HE SUFFERED

"Do you hear me?"

Mr. Christiansen is in a towering rage.

He has just returned from a four day out-of-town business engagement, anticipating a trip out into the country in the new car that was delivered the day before his departure from home.

In his absence Jimmy, aged 16, on the day after his daddy left had informed his mother that, in order to do his history assignment, he needed to consult some books in the library. As his older sister had taken the second car, it seemed the only way was for him to take the new Oldsmobile. His mother reluctantly agreed.

While Jimmy was sitting in the library, ostensibly studying but in reality talking with Esther Carol Powell, some student had backed into the side of the new automobile, leaving a horrible indentation that would test the skill of some body repairman.

Although Jimmy felt he had tactfully broken the news to his father, the elder Christiansen flew off the handle and began to yell at his son. He recalled his offspring's past irresponsibilities and then laid down an empiric edict—Jimmy was grounded until further notice.

Jimmy was displaying what he felt was commendable self-control, under difficult circumstances, and maintained a stony silence.

But rather than placating Mr. Christiansen, his

son's attitude infuriated the already frustrated father, and he flung out his challenge, "Do you hear me?"

Did Jimmy hear him?

He would have had to be deaf not to hear his irate father.

Everyone in the household heard Mr. Christiansen, the neighbors heard him, and, of course, Jimmy heard him. The problem was that Jimmy wasn't listening to his father.

Mr. Christiansen was hoping to change his son's behavior by shouting at him—a technique of punishing his erring offspring.

What was wrong with Mr. Christiansen's technique of discipline?

(1) He was setting the wrong model before Jimmy, teaching him by example to fuss and shout when upset.

(2) If punishment is to be effective it must be administered immediately, not a day or two after the event.

(3) Preeminently, Jimmy, by not paying attention, was punishing his father. His father thought he was punishing his son, but Jimmy was paying his daddy back at his own game. He was punishing his father by not paying attention.

One of the most telling forms of punishment is not to pay attention.

Why Not Try a T.O.?

If attention at its various levels is the greatest reward I can give another person, it follows that withdrawal of attention may be the greatest punishment that can be imposed.

This consideration provides the background for introducing T.O. or "Time Out."

Standish Lindemann has developed the annoying habit of punching his sister, Wilma, on the arm. Wilma, no long-suffering martyr, lets out a yell each time he hits her, and Standish chortles with joy at his sister's discomfiture.

Mrs. Lindemann has finally reached a place of utter frustration and feels she must do something about the situation. So she decides on the technique of Time Out and says to Standish, "I'm tired of the way you keep on teasing your sister, and I have decided to do something about it by using Time Out with you. Each time you tease your sister I am going to put you in the bathroom for three minutes."

When Mrs. Lindemann tells her friend, Mrs. Harrison, about her new technique, Mrs. Harrison smiles benevolently and says, "I'm sorry to have to tell you this, honey, but you are wasting your time. I tried that with my Jimmy; I sent him to his bedroom, and he let me know that he quite enjoyed the experience."

What was the difference between what Mrs. Harrison did and a good program of Time Out?

(1) Mrs. Harrison chose the wrong place for T.O. If Time Out is to be effective, the child must be placed in the most non-reinforcing environment. His room hardly fits this description. A completely bare room would be best of all, and failing this, some situation where there are no people, no toys, no TV, and no books. In most homes the bathroom is probably the best situation. Some kids say, "OK, I like it." Ignore this and continue on. Only time will tell. If they run the water or mess up, have a second penalty ready to use.

(2) Mrs. Harrison had spasmodically sent Jimmy "to his room." The Time Out program calls for consistency. The child must be sent to the bathroom "every time" he behaves in his objectionable way.

(3) Mrs. Harrison didn't have any specific time arrangement. She sometimes sends Jimmy to his room for periods of time that may last from thirty minutes to an hour. The main purpose of this is to get him out of her hair for a while. Some research has shown that Time Out may not need to be very long. Periods of time from one to five minutes may be very effective. This makes the kitchen timer

THE SKILL OF DISCIPLINE

The word "discipline" is related to "disciple" and has the predominant idea of teaching. Approach all disciplining from the educational perspective, and it will be far more effective.

Some Rules for Discipline

* *Stay calm and objective. If you get upset, you may be punishing yourself.*
* *Time the punishment carefully, so it is administered at the time of the undesirable behavior.*
* *Utilize clear warning signals—remember the pairing principle.*
* *Administer punishment consistently.*

Develop Your Ability with T.O. (Time Out)

Start from the premise that attention is the greatest reward, and withdrawal of attention will probably decrease undesirable behavior . . .

IF the right environment is used. A room with a minimum of reinforcers—preferably bare—the bathroom may have to do;

IF the timing principle is adhered to and "Time Out" is used every time the child misbehaves. Miss even once and you've flubbed it.

IF the duration is carefully regulated by using a timing device, such as a kitchen timer. A short time will do it.

important in the process. The parent sets the timer for the period so that when the bell sounds both parent and child know the period is up.

Sometimes good medicine tastes bad. Administering effective discipline involves time—taking time—timing it precisely.

The book of Proverbs is used so frequently to justify corporal punishment that we should note that proverbial discipline is always administered in the spirit of love. Making a comparison between God's love and a father's love Proverbs says, "Young man, do not resent it when God chastens and corrects you, for his punishment is proof of his love. Just as a father punishes his son . . ." (3:11–12). To parents there is a similar message about the place of love, "If you refuse to discipline your son it proves you don't love him, for if you love him you will be prompt to punish him" (13:24). The reason many parents do not discipline their children is they don't love their offspring enough to inconvenience themselves. As Proverbs says it in another place, "Discipline your son in his early years while there is yet hope. If you don't you'll ruin his life" (16:8).

DISCIPLINE IN PROVERBS

Proverbs 3:11–12	*Proverbs 22:15*
Proverbs 4:1	*Proverbs 23:13–14*
Proverbs 6:20–24	*Proverbs 29:15*
Proverbs 13:24	*Proverbs 29:17*
Proverbs 30:17	

13

THE PROVERBIAL METHOD OF CHILD REARING

Train up a child in the way he should go and when
he is old he will not depart from it.   Proverbs 22:6, KJV

Parents need help.

Parenting is one of the most complex and difficult tasks an individual ever put his hand to, and two inexperienced people, a father and a mother, have to struggle through the all-important task of rearing children so they will become responsible citizens of society.

Where can a parent find assistance for this difficult task? There's a good chance concerned and conscientious parents may turn to some system that will enable them to cope with their parental responsibilities. A great variety of methods are available—the Ginott method, the Spock method, the Piaget method, the Gessell method—but what about the Proverbial method?

We have already noted the way Solomon's reputation for wisdom was firmly established by his judgment in the case of the two women who came to him, claiming the same child. News of the king's wise verdict caused people to acclaim Solomon as the wisest of all kings. It was appropriate the incident should come to pass in a family setting. A member of a large family himself, he was the father of numerous children and when he gathered together the

179

sayings or proverbs that were so prevalent in his days it was natural that many of them should have to do with family life. The first nine chapters of Proverbs could be easily described as a manual of insruction for youth in which the father constantly speaks to his son, trying to prepare the young man for some of the temptations he will face in life and to impress the importance of wisdom on the youth's pliable mind.

Of course, all ages and stages of development are referred to in Proverbs, but a large proportion of the book is given over to the consideration of parents and their children. Apparently much of the discussion of Solomon and his wise men was concerned with parent-child relationships and the fruits of their debate are to be found in Proverbs, which presents us with what we might call the Proverbial method of childbearing. It involves four actions regarding children—understand them, train them, discipline them, love them.

UNDERSTANDING CHILDREN

Proverbs rings with the laughter of children and in this verse it agrees with much of the emphasis of modern psychological teaching about the nature of children. An idea is seen in two renderings of Proverbs 22:6, "Train up a child in the way he should go [and in keeping with his individual gift or bent] . . ." (The Amplified Bible). "Train up a child for his proper trade" (Moffatt).

The really peculiar thing about this statement in Proverbs is: it is an early acknowledgment of what is now referred to as individual differences generally thought of as a fairly recent insight into human-personality development.

In the early part of the nineteenth century, while trying to discover something about celestial mechanics, astronomers accidently stumbled on some of the most important factors in the functioning of individuals. While observing the transit of heavenly bodies it was noted that there was a difference in the reaction time of the observers. Psychologists became interested, and in short order considerable study was generated in area of individual differences.

Now has come a belated recognition of the area of individual differences. It should have always been clear, even with such phenomena as stones in a field—each is distinctive—how much more with humans. Two investigators put it like this, "Every man is in certain aspects (a) like all other men, (b) like some other men, (c) like no other men." An individual is like all other men to the extent that he shares a common heritage with a physical makeup akin to all other members of the human family. He is like some other men in the respect that he lives within a certain cultural group, feels the pressures of that society, and conforms, to a large extent, to what is expected from him by the group. However, in all of this he is unique, because no other person has undergone exactly the same experience as he. His heredity is unique, and the responses he makes to his environment are peculiarly his. The emphasis on individual uniqueness must overshadow theorizing about personality.

A sculptor friend of mine says his material "talks to him." Stone, wood talking? What he means is that the sculptor or the wood carver sits down and looks at the piece of stone or wood until he sees what it has in it—then he takes his chisel and tools and tries to bring out the hidden figure.

The teacher in the Medici sculptor school watched his new student carefully and noted the unusual talent the young man displayed. One day the teacher took his student for a walk on the Florentine hillside. As they walked he looked at his protegé.

At last the teacher spoke, "Admittedly I am not a

very great marble carver. But with you perhaps I can become a great teacher." The perceptive sculptor-teacher had perceived the young Michelangelo's remarkable gift.

Each child has a particular strength. We must discover this potential and develop it. Moffatt's translation catches the idea, "Train a child for his proper trade."

Wood workers look for the grain of the material they are using. They work with the grain, not against it. So, too, with these unique little lives that are put in our hands. We must discover the particular ability that they have and then deliberately set about to develop it.

TRAINING CHILDREN

Having reached an understanding about the child's nature and peculiar gifts, the next step is to decide just what should be done about developing these gifts. Solomon recommends "training," an idea that was in eclipse for a long time but is now coming back into its own.

To do the training adequately the parents need an objective. Matthew Henry with typical insight noted there are two ways in which the child can go. The first is the way he *would go*. That is doing just what he wants to do with no thought or concern for anyone else but himself. Thus, he is launched on the pathway that leads to destruction.

The other possibility is the way he *should go*. Inherent in this emphasis is the idea that the child is going to pass through a process of asocialization. He will spend years of his life learning how he has to relate to his parents, his siblings, and to society as a whole. These relationships with other people will become the basis for much of life.

In the accompanying chart we see a schematic presentation of how the systems of personality develop. These systems are generally referred to as the Id, Ego, and Super-Ego, the Id being the primitive self-seeking forces of personality, the Ego, the sense of developing self-awareness

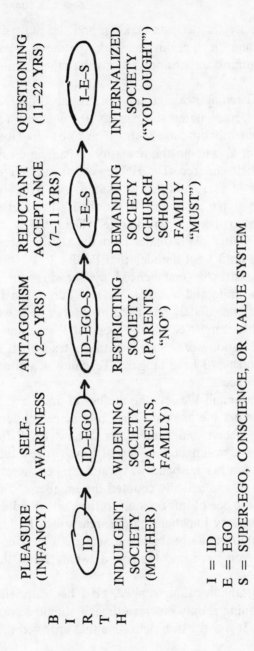

PLEASURE
(INFANCY)

SELF-
AWARENESS

ANTAGONISM
(2–6 YRS)

RELUCTANT
ACCEPTANCE
(7–11 YRS)

QUESTIONING
(11–22 YRS)

ID

ID-EGO

ID-EGO-S

I-E-S

I-E-S

B
I
R
T
H

INDULGENT
SOCIETY
(MOTHER)

WIDENING
SOCIETY
(PARENTS,
FAMILY)

RESTRICTING
SOCIETY
(PARENTS
"NO")

DEMANDING
SOCIETY
(CHURCH
SCHOOL
FAMILY
"MUST")

INTERNALIZED
SOCIETY
("YOU OUGHT")

I = ID
E = EGO
S = SUPER-EGO, CONSCIENCE, OR VALUE SYSTEM

and capacity for decision-making, and the Super-Ego, the
value system. In all of this the whole scheme of socialization
is of the utmost importance and involves the training of the
children.

Teaching is a constant note in the Bible. So in the
book of Deuteronomy the parents are not only reminded
about their monotheistic faith, "The Lord our God is one
Lord," but also about the necessity of passing on the message to their children. The Hebrew word has behind it the
metaphor of sharpening or whetting, so in *The Amplified
Bible* the statement reads, "You shall whet and sharpen
them so as to make them penetrate" (Deut. 6:7).

I didn't really understand the significance of this
statement until I got the idea that I'd like to learn to whit-
tle. My instructor commenced by showing me how to
sharpen a knife and a chisel. When I questioned the procedure he immediately reminded me that anyone who used
an edged tool must constantly work at sharpening it if he
were to do good work. So it is with the teacher. It is never
enough to say, "I have taught." Teaching is a continuous,
ongoing process.

Susannah Wesley, the mother of John and Charles
Wesley, in her lifetime gave birth to nineteen children, was
a gifted teacher, and part of her success came from her
patience and willingness to repeat things many times. On
one occasion her husband was watching her at work with
the children and actually counted the number of times she
repeated a piece of information to the same child. Samuel,
who had a very impatient nature, marvelled. At length he
could stand it no longer and commented, "I wonder at your
patience; you have told that child twenty times the same
thing."

Susannah calmly replied, "If I had satisfied myself
by mentioning it only nineteen times I should have lost all
my labor. It was the twentieth time that crowned it."

Long before professional educators had taught the idea, Susannah had learned that repetition breeds retention.

Few families in modern times have caught the attention of people in the way the Kennedy clan has. John, the youthful president, leading America through the "Camelot" years; Bobby, the brilliant attorney general following his brother as he, too, fell to the assassin's bullet. Presiding over this family like some matriarch is the unflappable Mrs. Rose Kennedy. Years ago Eunice Kennedy Shriver was asked about her mother's methods of rearing children. She said, "We were computerized at an early age, but fortunately by a very compassionate computer operator."

BELIEVING IN CHILDREN

Many activities are ventures of faith. The farmer, for example, goes out sowing his seed in the hope it will take root, grow, and produce; the minister preaches to his congregation and spreads the Word of God by faith. Teaching is also an exercise in faith, undertaken in the hope that teaching will some day pay off.

Any teacher must have a spirit of optimism. Some students have almost unbelievable potentialities. I look back over my own teaching career and remember having as listeners to my teaching, among others, an astronaut and a press secretary to the president of the United States. At the time when I spoke to them I little suspected what the future held for them.

Our proverb holds the reason why we should have such optimism when we teach our children, ". . . when he is old he will not depart from it." All teaching is a sowing in faith—particularly spiritual teaching. The child may depart from the teaching when he is young, he may depart from it in adolescence or adulthood, but "he will not depart from it when he is old." In later years some of the seeds sown will spring to life and grow.

A wise mother wondered about the story she should tell her child. If fairy stories, myths, or fables, could they not give her boy some wrong ideas about life? So she looked back on the history of the church and, as the little boy sat at her feet, she told the stories of the heroes of faith, the reformers, the missionaries, Martin Luther, John Calvin, Ulrich Zwingli, William Carey, and Adoniram Judson. Small wonder that when he grew to manhood he became Dr. W. W. Barnes, the great Baptist historian.

LOVING THE CHILDREN

All of this training and educating took place within the context of love, and the ideal proverbial home may not have had great financial resources, but it had love. "It is better to eat soup with someone you love than steak with someone you hate" (15:17). All the activities of the family including punishment were to take place within the context of love.

Piece by piece many of the functions of the family have been taken over by the all-powerful state. People often wonder what there is left for the family to do. The answer is the family *loves*. No impersonal state can ever do that.

In Proverbs the picture painted of a family is of a warm, loving unit where the members are familiar with many of the great ideas of Hebrew wisdom. This is the picture presented in the statement preceding the last chapter, which reminds us of the following wisdom as taught to King Lemuel "at his mother's knee." Reading this brought to mind the great essayist, Dr. F. W. Boreham, who tells about the evenings in his home when they had "Hassock Hour," a time when all the children sat on the floor around the mother, and she told them the stories that brought alive ideas later to become so important in the great writer's mind.

I once counseled with a mother who related the story of her foolish, wayward son. In her despair she looked at me with the question, "What will I do now?" I replied, "Mother, you'll go on doing what you've done all along. And when at last they throw him onto the ash heap of life, you will be there waiting to pick him up. You'll go on loving him."

The family must love. Not just with words, but with action demonstrations that show just how deep that love is.

The love situation was dramatized for me by Arthur Jennings, the leader of a communal group of kids known as the "Children of God." As I talked with him he presented a point of view that offended me, particularly when he asserted that the kids of the commune had no need of loyalty to their parents. As I argued with him, I asked with scorn in my voice, "How come you joined such a zany group of kids?"

In response he said, "All right, I'll tell you. I grew up here in Dallas in a good middle-class family. In my high school days I began to fool with dope and finally dropped out of school, joining up with a bunch of junkies. Then came news of the rock festival at Louisville. We went to that festival determined to try every type of drug experience available. I began to use LSD and it drove me out of my mind. I knew I was doing stupid things but couldn't help myself. I shouted and yelled and pushed my way into the sea of kids. They opened up before me and I plunged on through till I reached the other side of the field where a Volkswagen Bus stood with the door on its side open.

"I plunged into the bus where a group of kids grabbed hold of me and began to say many things like, 'Jesus loves you.' One of them climbed into the driver's seat, started up the engine, and drove out of the field and down the highway. Suddenly I had a violent reaction to the dope and began to throw up. I slipped and fell to the floor where I lay in my own vomit. Those kids pulled the bus onto the shoulder of the road and helped me out, removing my dirty clothes.

"One boy, I remember him well for he wore a clean white shirt, rolled it up into a ball and began to wipe down my soiled body. As he worked he said, 'God loves you. Jesus loves you. We love you . . .'

"Within myself I said, 'I've heard about love—now I've seen it.' "

That is the sort of love we must give in our families and not send our children off looking for love experiences in strange places.

PROVERBIAL CHILD REARING

Proverbs 1:8–9   *Proverbs 13:1*
Proverbs 4:1–3   *Proverbs 15:16–17*
Proverbs 6:20   *Proverbs 22:6*
Proverbs 10:1   *Proverbs 23:22–25*
          Proverbs 31:1

14

A JEWEL OF A WOMAN

If you can find a truly good wife, she is worth
more than precious gems.   Proverbs 31:10

A modern man who wants to care for his assets buys stocks, bonds, or insurance polices, or deposits his money in the bank where it is "insured safe," but the individuals who lived in Solomon's day had no such facilities available. Some of his assets may have been in herds and land, but when it came to hoarding away his money, he often used precious metals like gold and silver or jewels. Much of the jewelry he had hoarded represented his material possessions. In this passage the inspired writer tells us that the most valuable jewel a man can possess is not a diamond but his wife.

This figure of speech of a gem to describe a man's wife is all the more remarkable because it is used of a woman. Like most other cultures of antiquity, the Hebrews did not have a high view of femininity. The pious Pharisee went to the synagogue three times a day to thank God that he was not a Gentile, a leper, and above all, not a woman. This passage of Scripture is unique in all the Bible. The Old Testament repeatedly tells the story of masculine dominance. But this passage shows a picture of an ideal woman. When in a group of Americans the leader read this passage, one of the men exclaimed, "No woman could be that good." Interestingly there's no equivalent passage that tells us about the wonder of men.

The way jewels represented wealth and power in a bygone day was dramatized for me when I made a visit to the Tower of London. Jewelry accumulated by British royalty across the centuries is housed in this forbidding fortress. As I lined up with the crowds of other tourists to gaze upon the crowns, scepters, tiaras made of gold and encrusted with diamonds guarded by colorfully costumed attendants, I realized afresh how jewelry was used to impress the populace with the wealth and prestige of the king.

Solomon says this woman is a jewel, and this figure of speech has often been used to describe something valuable. I know a stockbroker who, when he talks about a security he feels is particularly good, will refer to it as "that little jewel," and the idea of comparing people to jewelry is to be seen in the lovely children's hymn.

> *When He cometh, when He cometh,*
> *to make up his jewels,*
> *All his jewels, precious jewels,*
> *bright gems for His crown,*
> *Like the stars of the morning, His*
> *bright crown adorning,*
> *They shall shine in their beauty*
> *Bright gems for His crown.*

Many jewels are made valuable by the manner in which they reflect light. The Australian opal is prized for its "fire," particularly bright-colored sparkling spots, and the diamond is enhanced by the way it is "cut."

As we consider this jewel of a woman we will note her life, like a diamond, has many facets, each of which reflects some distinctive part of her remarkable personality.

THE FACET OF HARD WORK

Although the writer uses the metaphor of a jewel, this gem of a woman is not just to be looked at and admired. In another portion of the book, Solomon warns about the problems of superficial beauty, "A beautiful woman lacking in discretion and modesty is like a fine gold ring in a pig's snout" (11:22). By way of contrast this woman not only looks, but she also "acts."

To back up his case the inspired writer produces a record of the various roles and activities that characterize this woman's life.

> PARTNER: She will not hinder him (her husband) but help him all her life. 31:12
>
> WEAVER: She finds wool and flax and busily spins it. v. 13
>
> IMPORTER: She buys imported foods, brought by ship from distant parts. v. 14
>
> MANAGER: She plans the day's work for her servant girls. v. 15
>
> REALTOR: She goes out to inspect a field and buys it. v. 16
>
> HORTICULTURIST: With her own hand she plants a vineyard. v. 16
>
> SHOPPER: She watches for bargains. v. 18
>
> PHILANTHROPIST: She sews for the poor and generously gives to the needy. vvs. 19–20
>
> SEAMSTRESS: She also upholsters with finest tapestry; her own clothing is beautifully made.
>
> ENERGETIC: Is never lazy. v. 27

For those of us who are more relaxed types, who enjoy the quieter form of life, even a reading of all this activity can leave us limp and worn. The woman is certainly the personification of an activist approach to life.

All this activity pays off in yet another way. While most people dread old age, it can be a particular threat to a woman. Recent studies have shown one of the ways to combat the onset of the aging process is to keep active. It certainly paid off with this woman of whom it is said, "She is a woman of strength and dignity and has no fear of old age."

THE FACET OF HUSBAND-WIFE RECIPROCITY

We have already noted the remarkable activity of this woman in her many enterprises. There were other women of action in the Old Testament like Deborah, Jael, and Naomi, but we know little about their husbands, and it may have been that in their marital relationship these women were the "better man of the two." Here, however, we note this woman's husband was no push-over; he occupied a high position. "Her husband is well known for he sits in the council chamber with the other civic leaders" (28:33). She matched his position of prominence and responsibility by the way she worked at home while he attended to the affairs of the city. Without her he would not have been able to accomplish all that he did.

This husband and wife are an excellent example of a working partnership, an instance of what the Scottish scholar Barclay calls, "The ethic of reciprocity," which comes into play as two people—husband and wife—interact with each other. It seems husbands and wives may need to relearn this idea today.

Today's Christian women are in the midst of an identity crisis, on the horns of a dilemma, trying to decide just what their role in life should be.

On the one hand we have the people who are from women's lib whose strident voices are crying out and saying women must have a higher status and referring to men as "male chauvinist pigs" and claiming, perhaps with some justification, that women have been discriminated against across the years. According to them, men should be challenged and fought so that women can take their place of rightful reciprocity. On the other hand, we have the people who are saying submit, submit, submit, and the idea seems to be that woman is a mindless sort of a person who can't make up her own mind and is unable to make her own decisions without the assistance and guidance of the "superior" male.

Look at this scenario. Jim and Joan Folsom are in their mid-thirties, the parents of three children. Joan is not only attractive in appearance but also has a vivacious personality. Although she graduated *summa cum laude* from college, when she married she gave herself wholeheartedly to the task of being a wife and mother. Jim, on the other hand, lacks many of Joan's qualities and has only been moderately successful in an advertising agency. Jim comes home one evening with eyes aglow to announce he has been in the showroom of a motor company looking at the new Mercedes-Benz. As he recounts his experience to Joan, he points out how important it is for him to make a good impression on his clients, and if he only had the Mercedes it would make all the difference in his work.

Joan knows they cannot afford to spend $12,000 on a Mercedes. What should she do?

A. Carefully point out all the reasons why they cannot possibly afford the Mercedes. She sits down with paper and pencil, figures all expenditures, and shows that it would be impossible to meet these payments. If after all this Jim still insists, she puts her foot down and tells him it is impossible and she will not go along with this idea, under any circumstances.

B. Indicate all the problems they will face if they buy the car, but if he still insists, agree to his going ahead with the purchase, and thank God for the automobile.

The answer is *B*. That is, if you are accepting this line of reasoning. Provided the husband does not propose something sinful, evil, or criminal, he has the last word. The wife has to learn to submit.

Apparently the cry of the new, unliberated, "dedi-

cated" Christian woman to her fellow women is "submit."
A woman is to be a poor mindless entity who after a minimum input into the marriage discussion gives into the
leadership of her all-powerful husband. She goes along with
what he says, no matter how unreasonable the proposition
might be.

Many a sensible woman today is saying, "A plague
on both your heads. I want no part or lot with either of
these positions. Let's get back to a biblical perspective."

The heart of this problem is presented in Ephesians
5. Notice how that chapter describes the relationship between husbands and wives. It starts off by saying, "Submit
yourselves one to another." Not just one person submitting
to the other, "Submit yourselves one to another."

Then comes the two-fold admonition, "Wives, submit yourselves unto your husbands as unto the Lord," followed by, "Husbands love your wives, even as Christ also
loved the church." There is the ethic of reciprocity. The
wife is to submit herself while the husband is to love with
the same sort of love with which Christ loved the church.

Now let us trace the passage on a little further, so
we can see that the argument has to do with three relationships—husbands and wives, as we have just noted, parents
and children, "Children obey your parents in the Lord"—
"Parents, provoke not your children to wrath"; owners and
slaves, "Slaves be obedient to your masters"—"Ye masters
do the same things unto them forebearing threatening."

Are we to gather from this statement about slaves
that the Christian message is that slaves must always submit to their masters, and thus put the imprimatur of the
Christian faith upon the most degrading institution known
to man? Certainly not. Paul was saying, in effect, "In the
interim, in this culture, until the day comes when the full
implication of the statement, that in Christ Jesus 'there is
neither bond nor free,' will be realized, put up with it—

obey your masters." When the time came Christians were in the forefront of the fighters against the institution of slavery.

A similar situation applied to women in husband-wife relationships. Women had a very low status in both the pagan and Christian communities. They are now beginning to move up the status ladder. One day the implication of the statement, that in Christ Jesus, "There is neither male nor female," will be worked out, but in the meantime, submit.

Note, too, how the husband is to behave towards his wife. He is to love her as Christ also loved the church and gave himself for it. Is this a dictatorial and demanding attitude towards his wife? Certainly not. The love of Christ was a giving love, and this is the sort of love a husband must have towards his wife.

This is a partnership, a His and Hers relationship in which both make a contribution.

HERS: "Her husband can trust her and she will richly satisfy his needs" (31:1). As a responsible wife she takes a load from her husband's shoulders, but she also realizes he has some very special needs, and she makes sure she supplies these.

HIS: Her husband praises her with these words, "There are many fine women in the world but you are the best of them all" (31:29).

Can you imagine how this sort of commendation coming from the lips of her husband would have motivated her?

Apiarists tell us all the new developing bees in their tiny cells are the same, but at a certain time it is necessary to raise a new queen for the hive. So one pupa is chosen and fed the royal gel. As it is fed with the royal gel, its cell is enlarged and the ordinary little bee grows to be a queen.

Want a queen in your home? Take an ordinary wife, feed her the royal gel of praise, and she will grow to be a queen.

THE FACET OF SUBTLETY

Jewish women had an unusual capacity to work around life's circumstances. Placed by their society in an inferior position, they came to realize they didn't have to make a direct approach to gain their objectives; they sometimes had to move in a circuitous fashion.

Why, then, should this remarkable passage occupy such a large place in the Old Testament, which is supposed to be the bastion of male superiority? Perhaps a clue may be found at the beginning of chapter 31. While some scholars have questions about the form of this chapter, let's take it as it is written. The first chapters of Proverbs come from Solomon, and he makes many references to his father, occasionally mentioning his mother. This chapter begins by telling us, "These are the sayings of King Lemuel of Massa, taught to him at his mother's knee" (31:1). So the important person here is King Lemuel's mother. She taught her son, got her message across through him. Never underrate the power of a woman to spread her influence through her children.

Colonial history provides us with a beautiful example. In the year 1900 A. E. Winthrop undertook a comparative study of two families, the Jukes and the Edwards. The Jukes family was descended from an immigrant from whom came 1,200 descendants. Of these, only twenty were ever gainfully employed. By the year 1900, the Jukes family had cost the state of New York $1,250,000 in welfare and custodial charges. This family had left behind a legacy causing trouble and became a source of expense for the taxpayers of the state.

For comparison Winthrop took the Edwards family. These were the descendants of Jonathan Edwards, the celebrated puritanical preacher and his wife, Sarah. From the

Edwards family there came thirteen college presidents, sixty-five professors, one hundred lawyers and a dean of an outsanding law school, thirty judges, sixty-six physicians and a dean of a medical school, eighty holders of public office, three United States senators, mayors of three large cities, governors of three states, a vice-president of the United States, and a comptroller of the United States Treasury. Someone said of the Edwards children that they entered the ministry in platoons and sent over 100 missionaries overseas. So great was the influence of the Edwards family that it has been called the "Gulf Stream of American Colonial Life."

When most people hear the name Edwards, they immediately think of Jonathan, the preacher of his famous sermon, "Sinners in the Hands of an Angry God," but little is ever mentioned about Sarah. Sarah worked in the background, but she exerted a tremendous influence on her children. This woman was subtly using her family as an extension of herself.

A similar situation obtained with Susannah Wesley. On one occasion in a letter to her husband, she said, "Though I am not a man or minister, I am resolved to start with my own children. So often we women have a unique opportunity working through our families and bringing to pass our purposes." And bring to pass her purposes, she did. As John Wesley looked over the ever-swelling members of Methodism he referred to Susannah as "The Mother of Methodism."

Many a mother by a subtle approach becomes the parent of a great host of dedicated, successful people.

THE FACET OF EXAMPLE

This passage, setting forth such an idealized picture of womanhood, was written in a special way. In Hebrew literature certain of the psalms, namely Psalm 119, and other writings of the Old Testament utilized an acrostic, each verse of the poem starting with a successive letter in the Hebrew alphabet. Proverbs 31:10–31 is written in this style. One writer calls it the "Alphabet of Wifely Excellence." Some Hebrew scholars think the acrostic form was used to make memorization easier.

If this be true, who memorized this poem? Was the little girl learning it so she could keep an ideal before her? Matthew Henry advances this idea, calling this passage "a looking glass for women." Or perhaps it was written for the boys, so they could early learn how they should treat their womenfolk.

Back to Jonathan Edwards' wife, Sarah. As the wife of the preacher, she had a special bench in the church. This bench was set apart from the others, so as her husband preached, everyone could see how Sarah was listening to him. If she dared to nod her head, or blink her eyes, or show them she was not attentive, then she was a cue to the whole congregation. She had to sit there and pay particular attention.

Wives, above everything else, should be good examples. I remember one minister's wife talking to her husband when he returned from speaking at a meeting. She said, "Well, honey, what did you preach about?" He said, "I preached about _____," "Oh, not that sermon again, it's got whiskers on it." Not only did she lack the element of subtlety, but she also discouraged her husband in his work.

We must all be examples. Some years ago we were living in Goulburn, Australia, where I was the chaplain of a psychiatric hospital. I used to come home in the afternoon and set some rabbit traps down in the bottom of a brick pit. It was a great big hole in the ground. At the bottom of the pit was a pool where rabbits used to come to drink water. I'd set the rabbit traps, and the following afternoon I'd have to come back, climb down the pit, and get the rabbits out of the trap. I usually took my son with me.

One afternoon it was cold and wet, so I decided to go by myself and slipped away without my small son. As I was climbing down the pathway leading to the bottom of the pit, I realized it was foolish to have come because the pathway was wet and slippery. About halfway down I stood hanging onto a tree growing from the side of the pit and wondered whether I ought to turn around and go back up. Suddenly a stone came rolling by. I looked up and saw that our little boy, Warwick, was walking down the track after me.

I called out for him to stop. "Warwick! Stop! Don't go any further! Don't go any further! Don't go any further!" I kept talking to him as I climbed up on my hands and knees. When I reached him I picked him up in my arms and carried him to the top of the pit. Though it was a cold day, I was bathed with perspiration, and a voice seemed to say to me, "That's the way it goes, John Drakeford. Where you go, your son goes. You've got to watch out. You're an example for him."

There's a little verse which goes like this.

> *His little arms crept 'round my neck,*
> *And then I heard him say,*
> *Four simple words I shan't forget,*
> *Four words that made me pray.*
>
> *They turned the mirror on myself,*
> *On secrets no one knew.*
> *They startled me, I hear them yet,*
> *He said, "I'll be like you."*

We will always be examples to our children.

PROVERBIAL TEACHINGS
ABOUT WOMEN

Proverbs 11:22   *Proverbs 21:19*
Proverbs 12:4   *Proverbs 27:15–16*
Proverbs 18:22   *Proverbs 31:10*
Proverbs 19:14   *Proverbs 31:30*
Proverbs 21:9   *Proverbs 31:29*

EPILOGUE

To conclude our study of wisdom and its application to family life, it is well for us to go back to the beginning of it all. As I have noted through this volume, wisdom for the Hebrews was a multifaceted experience. We may oversimplify the situation by saying that becoming wise involves a number of steps.

(1) *Determination.* Proverbs says, "Determination to be wise is the first step towards becoming wise," and adds for good measure, "and with your wisdom develop common sense and good judgment" (5:7).

(2) *Listening.* Much of the wisdom of the Hebrews came from the teacher-student relationship. So a second step in gaining wisdom is listening, "Listen and grow wise" (4:1).

(3) *Remaining cool.* The book of Proverbs abounds with warnings against violent emotional reactions. When the crises of life come it is important for us to remain calm, "A fool is quick tempered, a wise man stays cool when insulted" (12:16).

(4) *Practice within your family.* As we have noticed in our studies of Proverbs, the family is viewed as a labora-

tory within which the skills of living are learned and practiced. Wisdom is developed in this laboratory: "Love wisdom like a sweetheart, make her a beloved member of your
family" (7:4).

(5) *Have a correct attitude.* The importance of attitude is to be found in the statement of what some com-
mentators see as "the motto of Proverbs"—"The fear of
the Lord is the beginning of all knowledge" (1:7).

(6) *Remember the importance of a right relationship with a "Greater than Solomon."* Our Lord Jesus Christ
was familiar with Solomon but reminded his hearers that
ultimately Solomon pointed on to someone greater who was
yet to come. So he said, "And at the Judgment Day the
Queen of Sheba shall arise and point her finger at this generation, condemning it, for she went on a long, hard journey
to listen to the wisdom of Solomon; but one far greater than
Solomon is here [and few pay attention]" (Luke 11:31).

NOTES

Chapter 1

1. William Stevenson, *90 Minutes at Entebbe* (New York: Bantam Books, 1976), p. 140.

Chapter 4

1. Charles Nordhoff, *The Communistic Societies of the United States* (New York: Douer Publications, Inc., 1966), p. 408.
2. Karl and Jeanetta L. Menninger, *Love Against Hate* (New York: Harcourt, Brace, & Co., 1942), p. 261.

Chapter 5

1. Fred Belliveau and Lin Richter, *Understanding Human Sexual Inadequacy* (New York: Bantam Books, 1970), p. 219.

Chapter 6

1. "Crib Jobs," *Newsweek*. November 29, 1976, p. 39.
2. Jerry Vorpahl, "Get in Shape and Stay in Shape Like the Pros," *Holiday Companion*. October, 1976, p. 23.

Chapter 10

1. Helmut Thielicke, *Encounter with Spurgeon* (Philadelphia: Fortress Press, 1963), p. 235.

Chapter 11

1. Otto Ruhle, *Karl Marx, His Life and Work*. (New York: The Home Library, 1943), p. 323.